Lean,
Rapid,
and
Profitable
New Product Development

Other Best Selling Books by the Authors:

Winning at New Products: Accelerating the Process from Idea to Launch, Third Edition
(authored by Robert G. Cooper)

Product Leadership: Creating and Launching Superior New Products, Second Edition
(authored by Robert G. Cooper)

Portfolio Management of New Products, Second Edition
(authored by Robert G. Cooper, Scott J. Edgett and Elko J. Kleinschmidt)

Product Development for the Service Sector
(authored by Robert G. Cooper and Scott J. Edgett)

Generating Breakthrough New Product Ideas: Feeding the Innovation Funnel
(authored by Robert G. Cooper and Scott J. Edgett)

Best Practices in Product Innovation: What Distinguishes Top Performers
(authored by Robert G. Cooper, Scott J. Edgett and Elko J. Kleinschmidt)

All books are available for purchase at
www.stage-gate.com

Lean, Rapid, and Profitable

New Product Development

by Robert G. Cooper
and Scott J. Edgett

For more information on the concepts and tools introduced in this book, please visit the Product Development Institute Inc. at www.prod-dev.com

Special discounts for bulk purchase are available to corporations, institutions and other organizations. For more information, please call 905-304-8798 or email at info@prod-dev.com.

ISBN 1-4392-2460-9

First Printing, September 2005

Cover and Text Design by Laura Brady

Typeset in 11 point Adobe Garamond

CONTENTS

LIST OF EXHIBITS

CHAPTER 1

Understanding the Challenge

Effective Product Innovation –
The Number One Management Challenge

Have you ever wondered why some companies make product innovation seem so easy ... one big winner after another? For most companies, developing a steady stream of successful new products is a real challenge: New product productivity – output for a given input – is lackluster. Why? What's going wrong? And how can you improve and seek real productivity gains in product development?

Here is a startling fact: Productivity in product innovation in the top performing businesses is *five times* what it is in the average business – they get five times as much new product output for the same investment![1] And top performers get *12 times* the productivity as poor performers. How does your productivity rate by comparison? And how can you improve it by up to 12 times?

That's what this book is about: uncovering the keys to *maximizing your new product development (NPD) productivity*. In it, the results of our most

1

The Productivity Research That Underlies This Book

This book outlines Seven Key Principles that lead to higher productivity in NPD. Where did they come from? Since the 1970s, we have been undertaking studies of hundreds of new product projects, teams and companies, seeking the answers to the same question: Why are some so much more successful than the rest? These studies have been published in countless peer-reviewed scientific journals, and are probably the most complete set of investigations into new product success, failure and productivity anywhere. (Sources are in endnote 3.)

The most recent study, which is widely quoted in this book, is the study of best practices in product innovation undertaken with the American Productivity and Quality Center, and referred to as the CEK study. In it, a large number of businesses were investigated for both their NPD performance (measured in many ways) and the practices that lead to this performance. A select group of high-productivity businesses were identified, and their particular practices were investigated in more depth. From this, previous studies and numerous case studies, we are able to identify those factors that are most strongly correlated with productivity and performance in NPD. (See endnote 2.)

recent study into the drivers of new product performance[2] are presented (see box). This study builds on a long tradition of our NPD benchmarking studies.[3] In this book the seven most important drivers of increased NPD productivity are identified – the *Seven Principles of Lean Rapid and Profitable NPD*. And the next generation or version of Stage-Gate®* is outlined – an idea-to-launch process designed to drive winning new products to market quickly and efficiently.

---

* Stage-Gate® is the registered trademark of the Product Development Institue. See www.prod-dev.com.

Product innovation is vital to success

New products have a huge positive impact on company fortunes. New products currently represent about 30 percent of company sales in the U.S.[4] That is, products on the market for three years or less now make up almost one-third of businesses' revenues. A *Fortune* magazine study found the common denominator across the most admired companies in America to be "a passion for new products and new ideas".[5]

Product innovation is not only vital to success and prosperity, for some it's the only game in town. Look around: Companies that are doing well today – Procter & Gamble, 3M, Microsoft, Intel, Nokia, Toyota – invariably have an enviable stable of new products. P&G, for example, has become a veritable new product machine in recent years, in spite of the tough market situation often faced by consumer goods businesses. P&G occupied five of the top ten sales positions for new products in 2004.[6]

The message is getting through to senior management: A recent study by A.D. Little reveals "enhanced innovation abilities" to be the number one lever to increase profitability and growth among European companies, higher even than cost cutting and acquisitions-and-alliances (see Exhibit 1.1).[7] Similarly, a recent study by the Boston Consulting Group found that 90 percent of the companies surveyed indicated that generating growth through innovation has become essential for success and 74 percent of these executives indicate they will be increasing spending on innovation in 2005.[8]

Achieving positive results is an elusive goal

Achieving positive results in product development is no easy feat. Indeed new product failures seem to be more common than big successes. Look at the facts: Only one product concept out of seven becomes a new product winner; and 44 percent of businesses' product development projects fail to achieve their profit targets![9] Here are some more statistics from our most recent benchmarking study:

Exhibit 1.1 Levers to Increase Profitability and Growth

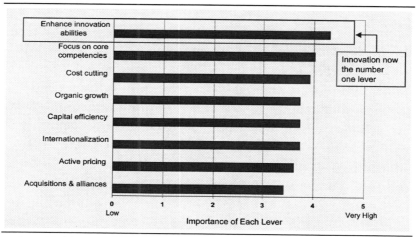

Source: A.D. Little Innovation Excellence Study, 2005

- 32 percent of businesses rate their NPD speed and efficiency as "very poor"
- Only 27 percent rate their NPD productivity as high – their profitability relative to how much money they spend
- 28 percent of businesses do not even measure their NPD performance results![10]

A comparison of the best NPD performing businesses to the average and worst reveals more insights into the challenges faced. Exhibit 1.2 shows performance results of the top, the average, and the poor performing businesses in NPD (here performance is judged on ten different criteria, including overall NPD profitability, impact on company sales and profits, on-time performance, and meeting sales and profit targets). Note that from Exhibit 1.2, *on every performance metric*, the top performers are doing exceptionally well – far better than the average and typically about 300 percent better than the poor performers. These are huge difference and they beg the question: What is it that separates the best from the worst – what are they doing so differently?

Another conclusion that can be drawn from Exhibit 1.2 is that, on many metrics, the average business is achieving very poor performance:

- Just better than half of NPD projects (56 percent) in the typical business meet their profit goals — 44 percent do not!
- Sixty percent of development projects are considered commercial successes, while 40 percent are either killed or fail commercially
- About half of the projects (51 percent) are launched on schedule, but 49 percent miss their launch date target
- And the slip rate — which captures how late projects are in reaching the marketplace as a percentage of scheduled time — is a dismal 35 percent on average.

The typical business, thus, faces major performance issues in product innovation. Much improvement in new product results and productivity is needed. Fortunately, the top performers provide a model for the rest of us. They show what is possible — that stellar results are within the grasp of any business and business leader — and they also provide insights into how to achieve these stellar performance results in product innovation.

Exhibit 1.2 How Businesses Perform in NPD

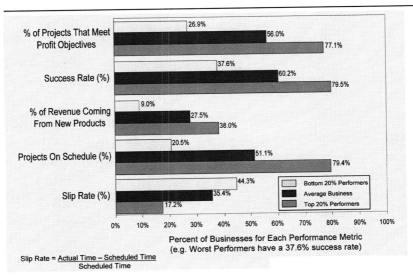

Source of data: CEK study, endnote 2

Why New Products Fail to Yield the Profits They Should

Perhaps the best place to begin the quest to improve NPD productivity results is to understand *why new products fail to perform*. Often, an understanding of past failures, problems and pitfalls leads to insights that ultimately result in corrective action. This is one premise of the process of continuous learning and the learning organization.

Why do so many new products fail to live up to their financial and sales expectations? Our data shows that almost half of development projects fail to meet their profit objectives,[11] and that as many as one-third of new products fail at launch![12] We compiled the following list of reasons and root causes for failure in an integration of research results from countless studies into new product outcomes,[13] and from many problem detection sessions held in companies.

1. Me-too, ho-hum or tired and trivial new products

The first reason for failure is that there is no search for competitive advantage. The new product idea is proposed, but the bar is never set high enough, and the project team develops yet one more me-too, ho-hum, tired and vanilla product, much the same as the competitors' product. There is *no compelling value proposition* for the users or customers and, given no reason to switch, they don't. And sales fail to materialize. One root cause is that management does not demand that project teams rise above competitors' offerings. The expectation is not there! By contrast, in one major consumer goods firm, the expectation is that the product will be "differentiated, unique, and deliver superior-to-competition performance"; otherwise the project is simply not done! A second cause is that many businesses have not built the "right stuff" into their new product processes – there is no emphasis on differentiated products and compelling value propositions. Indeed, if one were to diligently follow the typical firm's new product idea-to-launch guidebook, the result probably would be yet another vanilla product. Finally, for a variety of reasons ranging from pressure from the salesforce to a pervasive aversion to risk, the portfolio and development budget is consumed by an overabundance of extensions, modifications and tweaks – there's not much excitement and few blockbuster products in the development pipeline!

2. No front-end homework

Some businesses simply fail to do the needed up-front or front-end work on projects. The necessary due diligence on new product projects – the market study, the technical assessment, the financial analysis – is superficially done or not done at all. The result is that when it comes time to making key decisions – the product design freeze, or important investment decisions – there are many assumptions, but few hard facts. Frequently this lack of front-end work is because there is no time and no money to do the work, and very often people are too busy on other tasks. All are lame excuses. Another cause is the desire to reduce time to market. Cutting out the homework phase in order to save a few months' time sounds like a compelling argument if it were not for the huge body of evidence that argues otherwise – that poor or no homework actually lengthens, not shortens, cycle time and reduces new product success rates.

3. A lack of customer or user input and insights

Another reason why so many new products fail to reach their sales targets is the lack of understanding of the marketplace and the customer or user. The simple fact is that the project team develops a concept of what the product should be and do, often with very little real input from the marketplace. For example, there is little or poor voice-of-customer work done, and there are no visits to users by the project team to uncover insights into real needs and customer problems. Note that the "voice of the salesperson" is not a substitute for the "voice of the customer"! Also, if customer input is sought, it is limited to one or a few customers, and to immediate customers only – there is no attempt to broaden the customer base, nor to move down the value chain to listen to the customers' customers' voices. Further, as the product itself takes shape, and as various iterations of the product are crafted, there is little attempt to validate the product with the customer until too late in the process. In short, the customer or user is not an integral part of the development process. And so, when the product goes to field trials, to customer tests or even to launch, it is not enthusiastically welcomed by the marketplace.

4. Unstable product specs and project scope creep

Unstable product and project definitions, which keep changing as the project moves along, is the number one cause of delays later in the project. In this scenario, the project team moves the ball down the field, but someone keeps moving the goal-posts... and scoring a goal becomes next to impossible. For example, the project's scope changes: The project may begin as a simple one-customer request, and then becomes a multi-customer project. But before it is halfway through development, it's redefined again, this time as a new product line serving an entire market. Or the product definition and specs keep changing – the product requirements, performance characteristics and specifications are fluid, as different people who influence the project keep adding features or functionality even as the project nears the end of the development phase.

Sometimes unstable specs and scope creep are due to factors beyond the control of the project team; for example, a new competitive product entry, or the emergence of a new technology. But most often definition changes occur because of the arrival of *new information* – a salesperson indicates that the product needs an additional feature, or an executive sees a competitor at a trade show and wants the competition's function added, and so on. The "new" information is not really new at all. It could have, and should have, been available to the project team near the beginning of the project. The root cause is often traced back to number two above: a lack of front-end homework.

5. Functional silos and no real project teams

The lack of true cross-functional project teams is a major fail point in many new product projects. Indeed there is strong evidence that an effective cross-functional team is the number one key to driving cycle time down. But many companies get it wrong, as you'll see later in the book. In some companies, the project resembles a relay race: The Marketing Department "owns" the project for the first lap, and then hands it off to R&D for development; after R&D completes their phase or lap, they hand it off to Manufacturing, who throws it over the wall to the Salesforce for launch. In other businesses, which have attempted to field cross-functional teams, often the experience is marred: The team lacks members from all the key functions (for example, often the Manufacturing or Operations person does not join the team until well into development – too late!); the team leader is the wrong person and not really much of a leader at all; the team lacks cohesiveness and does not share a common vision of their project; some team members lack a strong stake in, and commitment to, the project; and team accountability is missing. What we really witness are "dysfunctional teams" rather than cross-functional teams!

6. Far too many projects in the pipeline – no focus

One of the greatest sins in product development is a senior management issue; namely, overloading the development pipeline. Far too many projects are approved at the early Go/Kill gates for the resources available. And there is no real attempt to deal with the resource issue later on, so projects keep getting added to the active list. The result is that every project is under-resourced and people are spread far too thinly. Projects look like strands of spaghetti: long and thin! And with so much multitasking (people working on far too many projects), many inefficiencies creep into the system, as much time is wasted switching from project to project. One result is that projects take far longer than they should, as the pipeline begins to resemble a logjam in a river. Another is that project quality starts to decline; for example, corners are cut, a needed market study gets skipped, the field trials are abbreviated, and so on, often with disastrous results.

7. A lack of competencies, skills and knowledge

In some businesses and projects, not only are people spread too thinly, there are not even the people available with the right skills, competencies and knowledge to undertake the project. Or the business is missing a key success driver, such as access to a marketplace or to a needed technology or technical skill. Sometimes the cause is that management approves the project, yet fails to understand that key resources and competencies are indeed missing and the project never should have been approved in the first place. Other times, this skills shortage is because the organization has down-sized so much that they have lost key technical and marketing talent. The people who are good at doing major and longer term projects, but are not needed for day-to-day marketing and technical work, are gone. Finally, the necessary partnerships and alliances are not in place. Management does not insist that outside business partners be found to bring the missing and needed skills to the table.

If you are typical, you've probably witnessed some or all of these seven reasons why new products fail to achieve their financial goals. No doubt, it is comforting to hear that other businesses suffer from the same maladies that you do. It is also reassuring to learn that many companies have identified these and similar causes, and are taking steps to overcome them. For example, a quick review of the seven causes of failure listed above reveals potential solutions – a stronger customer focus, better front-end work, more focus in the pipeline – which are built into prescriptions for improving results. As this book progresses, you will see how our Seven Principles of Lean, Rapid and Profitable NPD are designed to deal with many of these fail-points.

Speed is Vital to Success in Product Innovation

Yet another vital issue in product innovation is speed to market. As noted earlier, many businesses rate their speed and time efficiency as very poor, and on-time performance is mediocre. Thus, accelerating new product projects has been topical for over a decade, with many books and articles offering the secrets to time reduction. Many of these prescriptions work! But first, reflect on why speed should be important to you, and what role speed should play in your improvement goals for product innovation.

First, *speed yields competitive advantage*. Here the notion is that "first into the market wins". This is a valid argument for many businesses and industries, but it is not universal. For example, a major U.S. study revealed that "first in wins" is only true if the second entry is a same-as or parity product.[14] For example, if the first company launching a new computer disk-drive establishes the industry standards, then all successive products must be essentially me-too copies with no real competitive advantage. But that is not the case in most industries.

Nonetheless there is considerable evidence that order-of-entry and being first in does have a positive effect, although not nearly as strong as some myths suggest. Exhibit 1.3 shows that success rates decline somewhat for later products, dropping from about 70 percent for the first entrant to about 56 percent for last-in products – a 20 percent fall off. Similarly, rated profitabilities – whether or not the project meets or exceeds the expected profit – also drops with later order of entry. These effects of time and order-of-entry are not huge, however, and there is substantial evidence that "best in wins". Launching superior, differentiated products is a much stronger driver of new product profits than merely being first to market.

A second reason why speed to market matters is that *speed yields higher profitability*. There is solid evidence for this time effect. First, if one can get to market earlier, revenues are realized earlier. Since money has a time value, often the costs of delay – even just one month – are huge. Do the

Exhibit 1.3 Impact of Speed on Success Rates and Profitability

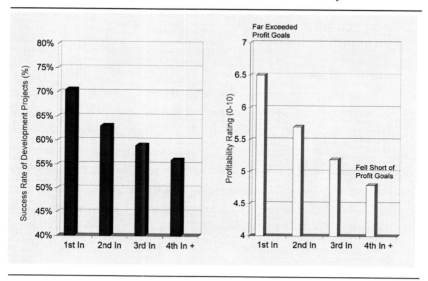

math: Postpone a revenue stream worth ten million dollars by one month and see what the cost is! Next, more revenue is realized. Many products have a fixed window of sales opportunity; if one misses the first year of sales because of tardiness, these sales are never recovered – a lost opportunity. Finally, there is anecdotal evidence that the longer a project lingers in development, the more inefficient and costly the project becomes.

Hitting the window of opportunity is a valid time-to-market objective. There may be a window in the market place: an unfilled void or a niche which is ripe for the taking. Or there might be a key trade show or buying season that all new products must be ready for. Or perhaps there are very demanding customers with their own rigid timelines. All are legitimate concerns, but none is a stellar reason for being "first in" or for "speed at all costs". Nonetheless, all are good reasons for being on time. And there is a huge difference between *being on time* versus *being fastest to market*.

On-time performance is a major problem, however. Note from Exhibit 1.2 earlier that the average slip rate (time slippage as a percentage of scheduled time) is 35 percent. For example, a 35 percent slip translates into a business promising 12 months to deliver, but delivering in 16 months. Note that the best companies cut this slippage in half, down to 17 percent!

A final reason to emphasize speed to market is that *things change*. Markets, competition and technologies are all fluid and change at lightening speed. A project is begun, based on assumptions and knowledge about the technology, market needs and the competitive landscape as it was at the beginning of the project. By the time the product reaches the market, however, everything has changed and many of the original assumptions are no longer valid. The longer it takes to get to market, the greater the likelihood that everything has changed! Thus, automobile companies that traditionally take over five years to design, develop and launch a new car – versus 20 months at Chrysler – are at a decided disadvantage. The car is already out-of-date as the first one rolls off the assembly line!

There are many valid reasons why you and your leadership team should be focused on time to market and cycle time reduction. But words of warning: There is also a dark side to the relentless pursuit of speed, as you'll see below.[15] So don't become a speed demon. The ultimate goal is profitable innovation, not a basket full of fast failures and mediocre launches!

The Executive's Dilemma: Faster, Better, Cheaper

Executives everywhere are being urged by their Boards to deliver a steady stream of new product winners, and sooner rather than later. Quite clearly, investors have figured out that cost cutting and acquisitions are not the way to sustainable, profitable growth. As markets mature and competition increases, products become commodities and margins inevitably shrink. Cost cutting can keep up with commoditization for only so long. Acquisitions are one way to deal with the growth goal, but these are expensive, do not always work (witness the recent merger of HP and Compaq), and often do not provide access to the hoped-for innovative products with new life.

So the message is "innovate or die!" One issue is that the goals of "faster, better, cheaper" are frequently in conflict. As one insightful executive declared: "You can have two out of three – take your pick. But you cannot have all three". [16]

"Better" usually means better executed, as well as bigger and more profitable new products. So the quest for winning and major new products is on. One challenge is that many firms' development portfolios currently are consumed by small, incremental developments with low value to the company. There are many reasons for this, including a short term orientation and an over-emphasis on speed to market; being overly reactive to every customer and salesperson's requests; an aversion to risk; a shortage of resources required to do major projects; and too heavy a financial focus with an over-emphasis on financial criteria to select projects. [17] Thus, finding, resourcing and executing these major and profitable new products is not as easy as it seems!

A second push is for "faster", which translates into a reduction in time-to-market. While cycle time reduction is an admirable goal as noted above, often the results of trying to reduce time-to-market have unexpected and negative consequences. For example, many maladies have been attributed to an overzealous pursuit of speed. Cutting corners on projects, dumbing-down projects, doing only the "low hanging fruit" projects, and poor team morale have all been blamed on excessive emphasis on cycle time reduction. [18]

In recent years, the goal of cycle time reduction has been achieved in the U.S., but not in the intended way! A recent PDMA study shows that new product times-to-market have decreased dramatically from 41.7 months to 24 months in a decade. [19] But the reasons are not that product developers have become more efficient; rather, businesses are simply not undertaking the challenging, step-out and significant innovations and new products they once did[20]. They are focusing on incremental improvements that inherently take less time but also make less money. One business unit executive put it bluntly: "Unless it contributes to this quarter's bottom line results, don't do it!", as he urged his people to focus strictly on near term results and commit nothing to the longer term.

A third push has been for *making the numbers* and short-term profits. That has led to many cost-cutting initiatives within firms and the desire to do product development more cheaply. To meet short-term financial goals, business management faced two choices: They could do what was good for the business for the longer term, or resort to short-term maneuvers – cost cuts and resource freezes – in order to achieve the immediate goals set by corporate headquarters.[21] As one exasperated business unit General Manager declared (and this is typical): "I grew the business – both top line and bottom line – by 20 percent last year. But I'm being 'punished' by Corporate [head office] for doing this. To achieve this growth, I had to increase operating costs – we hired more technical people – and so my operating ratios suffered. I'm being measured and incented all wrong!"

This preoccupation with short term profitability and cost cutting has ultimately resulted in the *resource crunch* in many organizations. Simply stated, managements have "hollowed out" the company in a zealous attempt to make the numbers. And the immediate result is that in many major corporations, that have been displaying superb operating results, the ability to innovate has been lost – there's no one left to do the work! The end result is that projects are thinly staffed, corners are cut and execution suffers. With too many projects for the available resources, projects end up in a queue and take too long to get to market. And when they are finally launched they underperform, mostly due to shoddy work done in the earlier stages. And, then, there is even more pressure to cut costs, so the downward spiral gets worse.

The goal is *lean, rapid and profitable* product innovation. But these major drivers for performance – more profitable projects, but faster to market, and using the same or fewer resources – have placed business managers in a serious dilemma. Focusing only on "lean" or cutting costs alone can lead to resource reductions and cost cutting with potentially negative consequences on NPD results, as noted above. A strict focus on accelerating projects also has many negative consequences. Similarly, over-emphasizing major and profitable projects may lead to many long-term initiatives that never get to market; or, this may simply be an elusive goal, given businesses' preoccupation with tweaks, modifications and extensions.

If the goal is really *lean, rapid and profitable new product development*, all three goals must be considered together and holistically. The solution, of course, is to focus on *maximizing NPD productivity* – maximizing the output, measured in profits and sales, for a given level of resource commitment. This need for a more balanced, integrated and holistic approach – balancing the goals of lean, rapid and profitability – is why we focus on *NPD productivity* rather than on any one element such as "lean", and it is what this book is about. You'll see more about measuring NPD productivity in the next chapter, and how to seek major gains in NPD productivity in the chapters that follow.

A Roadmap of this Book

We begin our quest for the secrets to improved product innovation with a look at what productivity is in NPD in the next chapter, and we witness some benchmark results from companies. The principles of Lean Manufacturing also have something to offer product developers, and are reviewed. Finally, Chapter 2 introduces our *Seven Principles of Lean, Rapid and Profitable New Product Development*.

Chapter 3 focuses on gaining competitive advantage in the marketplace, and it lowers the microscope on the first three principles. We provide the details of what these three principles are, how they work, and what impact they have on productivity improvement. Chapter 4 continues the same theme, but with an emphasis on getting the project to market quickly but effectively, and provides insights into the next two principles.

One way to make big gains in productivity is to be more judicious about which investments you make. Thus, the topic of portfolio management is the main theme of Chapter 5 and Principle Number 6. Here we explore ways to improve your portfolio management system, resource allocation, project selection and project prioritization methods to increase your overall NPD productivity.

All of these six principles are integrated and lead to Principle Number 7, the next generation idea-to-launch system, the topic of Chapter 6. Here, in addition to the six principles, we also see ways that firms are improving the way they move projects to market by using a more flexible, efficient and adaptable process.

The last chapter provides a quick summary, some implementation tips and hints, and outlines actions you can take.

So read on, and get set for a journey where you learn about the principles of *Lean, Rapid and Profitable New Product Development*, and how your business can maximize its NPD productivity.

CHAPTER 2

Focus on NPD Productivity

The Concept of Productivity in Product Innovation

The concept of productivity is simple: It is output over input or "the most bang for the buck". For example, when one talks about "productivity gains in the national economy", one measures increase in Gross National Product (GNP) per capita: Here, GNP or the sum total of all goods and services produced is the output, and "capita" or people are the input.

More specifically in business, productivity translates into maximum goal achievement for given resource commitment or spending. In the field of product development, productivity at the business unit level is most often defined as output (measured as new product sales or profits) divided by input (measured as Research and Development (R&D) or NPD costs and time), as shown in Exhibit 2.1.

19

For example,

Productivity in NPD is…

- profitability from your business' product innovation
- for a given R&D spending level.

NPD productivity is down

The concept of NPD productivity is so new that there are few hard numbers on results achieved in industry. Indeed, our recent benchmarking study reveals that almost no companies measured or reported their NPD or R&D productivity as a business metric.[1]

There is some evidence, however, that NPD productivity is heading in the wrong direction. In the U.S., a recent PDMA best practices study reveals that sales from new products are off in a period when R&D spending has remained constant. More specifically, new product sales fell from 32.6 percent of total company sales in the mid 1990s to 28.0 percent in 2004.[2] At the same time, R&D spending in the U.S. remains relatively unchanged; for example, 2.76 percent of GNP in 1985 versus 2.82 percent in 2001. So that's a 14 percent drop in output per spending in less than a decade – quite a dramatic downward shift in NPD productivity.

These significant decreases in just a handful of years are cause for concern. What's going on? New products remain a major component in corporate revenue and profits. But something is happening to make them a smaller portion of that revenue and profit.[3]

There is no evidence that people are doing a worse job today – poor market studies, bad launches, or deficient design and development work. Indeed, a comparison of the quality of execution of key activities between 1985 and today – from initial screening through to market launch – reveals no change in quality ratings.[4] On the other hand, product developers have not improved at all when most pundits believe they should have, so that is a second major cause for concern.

The one factor that does show a dramatic change, however, and that explains the decrease in profitability and impact is *the balance in the portfolio of projects undertaken today versus 1990.* Simply stated, today

Exhibit 2.1 Productivity in New Product Development Defined

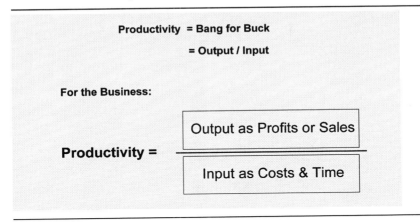

businesses are preoccupied with minor modifications, product tweaks, and minor responses to salespeople's requests, while *true product development has taken a back seat.*[5] (More on the critical challenge of seeking to rebalance the portfolio and improving its productivity in Chapter 5.)

Major gaps in productivities

One recent Arthur D. Little study in Europe does provide insights into productivity by industry. The study looked at output – measured by 5-year sales from new products as a percentage of company sales – and input, measured by R&D spending, also as a percentage of company sales.[6] Exhibit 2.2 shows the productivity results. One startling conclusion is *how much productivity varies by industry,* from a high of 14:1 in consumer goods to a low of about 2:1 in the pharmaceutical industry. A second revelation is *how low the productivity numbers are.* Note that output was measured by sales *over five years!* On the other hand, recognize that the R&D number reported is heavily overstated as far as new products are concerned, as less than half of R&D spending goes to new product development (much of R&D goes to "other things", such as process development, meeting regulations and solving customer and production problems). Still, the low-productivity numbers come as a shock. And, in case the North American reader dismisses these numbers as being reflective of an unproductive Europe, recognize that the R&D spending figures broken down by industry in Europe are almost identical to U.S. data; that the industry average NPD productivity in the U.S. is only somewhat higher than that for Europe (we do have U.S. data on that); and that the PDMA results showing productivity heading in the wrong direction are also U.S. based!

When one compares the most productive companies (the top 25 percent of businesses on this metric) versus the least productive (the bottom 25 percent of businesses), the results are even more provocative (see Exhibit 2.3). There are huge differences in productivity between the best and worst performers – on average, almost a 1200 percent difference! And in some industries, such as pharmaceuticals, the differences are even greater. For example, the top 25 percent of pharmaceutical firms are 31 times more productive in product development than the bottom 25 percent!

Exhibit 2.2 NPD Productivity — New Product Sales to R&D Spending

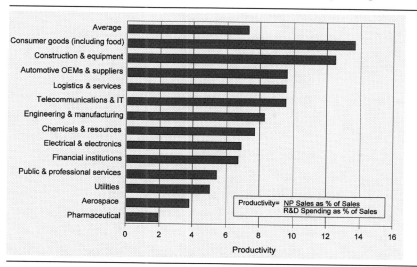

Source: Based on data from Arthur D. Little Innovation Excellence Study, 2005.

Exhibit 2.3 NPD Productivity — Best, Worst and Average Companies

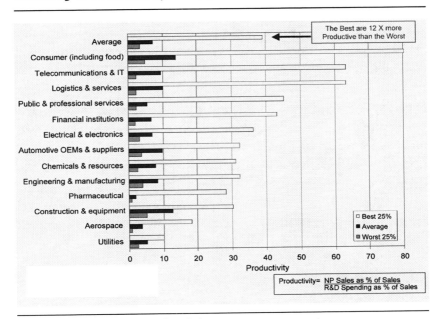

Source: Arthur D. Little Innovation Excellence Study, 2005.

These productivity differences between top and poor performers are huge and lead to the obvious question: Why? What is it that these high-productivity businesses do so differently? And can your business learn from them? Later in this book, we'll take results from our most recent benchmarking study that looks at best performers in terms of productivity versus worst performers, and gain insights into what the secrets to high-productivity are – what the best performers do so differently.

Productivity measured at the project level

So far, we have focused on productivity at the company or the business unit level. But a business' NPD productivity is the aggregate or sum of all the productivities of its individual new product projects. We might argue that if you wish to improve your productivity overall, the key is to increase the productivity of each individual NPD project.

Ironically, for some years, some R&D managers have measured *project productivity* by way of a little-known metric called the *productivity index*.[7] Initially, this productivity index was a tool to help research managers rate and rank projects – to yield project prioritization in the pipeline (for a definition of the Productivity Index, see Exhibit 2.4).

The strength of this productivity index is that it is a metric that ordinary employees can measure, can focus on, and through their actions, can improve. For example, suppose the goal in a new product department is to *increase the productivity of every project* underway by 20 percent. Project teams can then work on meeting this goal using various problem solving approaches, project best practices and project management techniques, and, if all project teams are successful, the effort will indeed increase the total productivity of the business's overall product innovation effort by 20 percent!

Another route is to be *more selective* in the projects that are approved for development, the goal being to select only those projects whose productivity index exceeds the productivity index of an average project in the current portfolio by 20 percent. Again, if successful, the result would be a major increase in NPD productivity for the business. Thus, this apparently simple productivity index has great potential leverage and power.

Lean Manufacturing and How It Applies to Product Innovation

Lean Manufacturing concepts have been widely employed on the factory floor to improve productivity. The use of the term "Lean" in a manufacturing environment describes a philosophy that incorporates a collection of tools and techniques into business processes to optimize time, human resources, assets and productivity, while improving the quality level of products and services to their customers. Becoming "Lean" is a commitment to a new journey, to a process, and to a considerable learning experience.[8]

Exhibit 2.4 Measuring NPD Projects With the Productivity Index

At the NPD project level:

$$\text{Productivity} = \frac{\text{Profit From a Project}}{\text{Cost \& Time To Do Project}}$$

$$\text{Example: PI*} = \frac{\text{Forecast NPV From Project}}{\text{Person-days to Complete Project}}$$

*Called the Productivity Index

A comparison of a Lean enterprise with a traditional mass-production organization is provided in Exhibit 2.5.[9] In a Lean enterprise, the organization is focused on the customer and on gaining competitive advantage by being customer focused rather than on economies-of-scale and producing standard products. The Lean enterprise is a flat organizational structure rather than the traditional hierarchical, chain-of-command, military structure, with excellent information flow vertically and horizontally. And the Lean organization is a smart system, with more intelligent components, featuring continuous learning and experimentation. By contrast, the traditional organization assumes dumb tools, a division of labor (bosses and workers), with the workers mechanically following orders and no learning at the worker level.

Lean Manufacturing focuses on removing waste in the manufacturing process, and is built on six main principles:

1. Zero waiting time – no queues in the process
2. Zero inventory
3. Scheduling based on internal customer pull instead of push system
4. Batch to flow, which means cutting batch sizes
5. Line balancing
6. Cutting processing times (by removing waste in each operation).[10]

Exhibit 2.5 Concepts in Lean Manufacturing Can Help

Comparison of requirements for mass and lean enterprises

Areas Affected	Mass Production	Lean Enterprise
Business strategy	Product-out strategy focused on exploiting economies of scale of stable product designs and non-unique technologies.	Customer focused strategy focused on identifying and exploiting shifting competitive advantage.
Organizational structure	Hierarchical structures that encourage following orders and discourage the flow of vital information that highlights defects, operator errors, equipment abnormalities, and organizational deficiencies.	Flat structures that encourage initiative and encourage the flow of vital information that highlights defects, operator errors, equipment abnormalities, and organizational deficiencies.
Operational capability	Dumb tools that assume an extreme division of labor, the following of orders, and no problem solving skills.	Smart tools that assume standardized work, strength in problem identification, hypothesis generation, and experimentation.

Source: Endnote 9

To realize these six principles, Lean Manufacturing heavily emphasizes problem solving and continuous learning.

The question now becomes: How can these six principles of Lean Manufacturing be applied to product innovation? It may not be evident to you how "batch to flow" or "line balancing" can be directly introduced to an innovation process or project. Some Lean principles do apply easily; for example, "zero waiting time" translates into "do fewer projects and don't overload your innovation pipeline".

The main contribution of Lean Manufacturing to product innovation is the philosophy and approach to waste and time reduction. Another contribution, but beyond the scope of this book, is designing for manufacturability (or Design for Six Sigma, DFSS). Consider our definition of productivity in Exhibit 2.6. The denominator is where most of Lean's principles apply: removing cost and time spent on product development in order to improve NPD productivity.

Exhibit 2.6 The Components of NPD Productivity

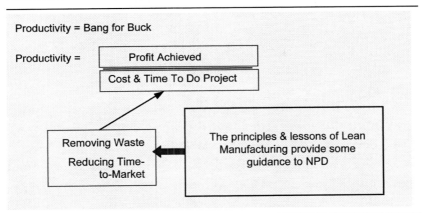

Words of warning

Lean can be thought of as trying to get the enterprise in shape for competition, much like an athlete training to get in shape for the big race. Getting in shape includes "leanness", but focusing only on losing weight will not win the race. The athlete must adopt a more balanced and multi-dimensional approach that includes fitness and skills through exercise and practice.[11]

An over-zealous application of the principles of Lean Manufacturing to product innovation can do much damage. For example, too heavy an emphasis on waste removal and cost reduction – a strict focus on the denominator in Exhibit 2.6 – may actually damage product innovation by forcing a shift to smaller, lower-risk and easier-to-do projects. Costs are reduced, cycle times are dramatically shortened and people and tasks eliminated, but the overall and longer-term effects are disastrous, as these projects fail to generate significant profits. In short, by attacking the denominator in Exhibit 2.6, we also lower the numerator and hence gain nothing! That is why we broaden the goal from simply one of "Lean" to a goal of *Lean, Rapid and Profitable*... that is, improving productivity, and not just cutting costs, waste and time. As T.R Browning, Senior Project

Manager at Lockheed Martin Aeronautics points out: "In an effort to improve company operations and their results, more firms are applying the principles of "Lean" not only to Manufacturing but to systems engineering processes. Too often, this is done with a shallow understanding of Lean and/or without a systems view, in which case Lean creates new problems and tensions".[12]

When applying the principles of Lean Manufacturing to product innovation, you must do so carefully and selectively. Product innovation is a very different type of process than Manufacturing: It is project-based rather than a continuous flow, with the work much less repetitive and predictable. By contrast, Manufacturing is relatively routine – "one car after another coming down the production line". Next, product innovation is much more variable and uncertain, and is characterized by missing and fluid information, especially near the beginning of projects. The result is that product innovation is more difficult to plan and requires more creative and abstract thinking to cope with this uncertain and incomplete information. The process has much tougher decisions built in along the way than does the typical production process (for example, Go/Kill decisions – project quality is more difficult to measure than product quality).

Some parallels do exist between Manufacturing and product innovation; thus, some Lean Manufacturing principles do cross over. The point is that a naïve and direct application of the principles of Lean Manufacturing to product innovation is wrong, because the process and environment is so different from the Manufacturing process and environment. We recommend that you apply the Lean principles *selectively* to product innovation, but most importantly, move beyond Lean and *focus on productivity improvements in product innovation.*

Introduction to the Seven Principles of Lean, Rapid and Profitable NPD

Our principles of lean, rapid and profitable NPD, with the goal of improving NPD productivity, have been developed from a long line of research investigations (many undertaken by the authors), culminating in our most recent benchmarking study.[13] Each of the Seven Principles is *very much fact-based*; that is, we can show from research investigations that businesses or project teams that employ each principle *achieve superior performance results*. For example, in the sections to follow, you will see some bar chart results from the recent benchmarking study. What these bar chart results show is that best performing businesses do employ each of these Seven Principles far more so than the rest of businesses, and that poor performers in particular tend to ignore these principles. In addition, most of the principles have been well-researched in previous studies that focused on large samples of individual new product projects and project teams, and the results were clear in those studies as well: The teams that employed each principle or practice were more successful! Note that our research results have been widely published in legitimate and refereed scientific journals, lending credibility and authenticity to what we present below;[14] we are not simply reporting on, or speaking from, a handful of experiences, anecdotes, case studies and home-grown research here.

The message is very clear: If you want to be a best performer in product innovation, do what the best performers do: Adopt and embrace these Seven Principles! Read on and gain a quick overview of the seven most important practices – our principles of *Lean, Rapid and Profitable Product Innovation* – that lead to improved performance and higher NPD productivity. They are summarized in Exhibit 2.7.

1. Customer focused

Developing and delivering new products that are differentiated, solve major customer problems, and offer a compelling *value proposition* to the customer or user is the number one key to product innovation success and profitability. But conceiving such unique, superior products is no easy feat. It begins with a thorough understanding of the customers' and users' unmet and often unarticulated needs through in-the-field voice-of-customer work. And there is more: The customer or user must be an integral part of the entire development process from scoping, through product definition, development and right to validation and beyond.

2. Front-end loaded

Due diligence in the early days of a new product project pays off! Ask the venture capitalist. A good dose of the right up-front homework pays for itself ten-fold in terms of saving time and also higher success rates. Smart management teams demand and get the right front-end homework done on projects, the right market, technical and business assessments. This homework is not excessive – it is designed to yield just enough of the vital information to make a Go-to-Development decision, and to define the product and project sufficiently to proceed. The right homework is also instrumental to yielding a winning product and project definition.

3. Spiral development

Things change! Often a project team charges into development with a product definition based on information that was right at the time, or which they thought was accurate but wasn't; or the market shifted; or a competitive product was introduced. But the product is developed and, when launched, is not quite right for the market. By contrast, smart development teams practice *spiral development*. They develop a first version of the product, perhaps a virtual prototype. And they test it with the customer, seeking feedback, which they then use to produce the next and more complete version, perhaps a working model or protocept. These fast-paced teams remove unnecessary work and move quickly to a finalized product by building a series of iterative steps or "loops" – "build-test-feedback-and-revise". These iterative loops are built into the entire development process from scoping right through the development phase and into testing. When sketched on a flow diagram, these loops appear like spirals, hence the name "spiral development".

4. A holistic approach driven by effective cross-functional teams

Product innovation is very much a business function (not an R&D activity) and team-based endeavor. And the core team – an effective cross-functional group – is the number one key to cycle time reduction and to getting to market on time. Effective cross-functional teams are comprised of key players drawn from different parts of the organization, each with an equal stake in and commitment to the project. They remain on the field from end to end, not just for one phase of the project. Team accountability – results measured against success criteria – is also key to effective team performance. The team is led by a carefully-selected champion or captain, driving his or her project down the field to the goal-line in an entrepreneurial fashion. How the team is organized, the team composition, the roles and authority of key players, and the choice and role of the team leader or captain make all the difference between efficient time-driven projects and those that languish and take forever.

5. Metrics, accountability and continuous improvement

You can't manage what you don't measure. Many businesses are guilty of not measuring their new product results. For example, it is not clear whether a specific project was a success – met its profit targets or met its launch targets. And often new product results for the entire business are missing – for example, total profitability generated annually from new products. Without metrics in place, project teams can not be held accountable for results. And learning and continuous improvement is next to impossible.

Top performing businesses put metrics in place. They measure how well individual projects perform by building a post-launch review as well as gate reviews into their idea-to-launch process. Here, project teams are held accountable for delivering promised results against these metrics. And when gaps, problems and weaknesses are identified, problem solving sessions are held that focus on root causes; corrective actions designed to stop future recurrence are identified. So, learning and continuous improvement becomes an integral and routine facet of the development process – every project is executed better than the one before.

6. Focused and effective portfolio management – a funneling approach, and putting the resources in place

Most companies have too many development projects underway, and often the wrong ones. That is, they fail to focus, spreading their resources too thinly across too many initiatives; thus their project choices result in the wrong mix and balance of development projects in the portfolio. The result is projects take too long and there are too many low-value projects. Every development project is an investment. And, like stock market investments, these development investments must be carefully scrutinized and focused through an *effective portfolio management system*. This is achieved through a funneling approach: Start with many solid new product concepts and successively remove the weak ones via a series of gates. The result is fewer projects, but higher value projects to the company, and a significant improvement in productivity.

The resources must also be in place. Securing adequate resources for projects is partly the result of an effective portfolio management system, which ensures that the pipeline is not overloaded. Another facet of correct resourcing is planning: estimating the resource requirements correctly; projecting how long key tasks will take; and preparing an effective "go-forward" plan. Finally, the needed resources – people and money – must be secured at the important gates: gates are not just Go/Kill decision-points, they are also *resource allocation points*.

The integration of these principles then leads to...

7. The NexGen Stage-Gate® Process – a flexible, adaptable, scalable and efficient product innovation process

Many idea-to-launch processes contain too much bureaucracy, time wasters and make-work activities. Even worse, they are rigid procedures, demanding too much paperwork, forms, meetings and committees, regardless of the project. By contrast, smart companies have streamlined their product innovation processes, removing waste and inefficiency at every opportunity (the Kaizen method). Their processes are also flexible and scalable, to suit the needs and risk levels of different types of projects – for example, large high-risk projects versus smaller, well-defined ones. They build into their processes the necessary flexibility, capability and systems to work with outside organizations, building their network of partners, alliances and outsourced-vendors into the process. The most progressive firms have also *automated* their idea-to-launch processes. And their processes are adaptable and dynamic – they adapt to the changing situation and fluid circumstances of the project as the project evolves, and as new or more accurate information becomes available.

Comparison with other principles

Progressive companies have also developed their own principles of effective product innovation. One of the most intensely-researched companies is Toyota, and indeed several books and reports on Lean product innovation are based on Toyota.[15] For comparison, we list Toyota's Product Innovation Lean Principles in Appendix 1.[16] There are many parallels to ours in their list, but some obviously apply only to the automotive industry.

There are also other views on what Lean product development is. One thing that becomes apparent is that Lean product innovation means different things to different people.[17] For example, in one major

European company, Lean product development essentially boils down continuous improvement designed to remove waste.[18] At Apple, it means cycle time reduction via a global new product process that clarifies roles, nails down the timeline, and maps out the process end to end.[19] And others more correctly view Lean product development a little more broadly, for example in terms of a more holistic and multi-dimensional set of prescriptions[20] ranging from portfolio management to pipeline management to managing development partners.

Moving Forward

What do each of our Seven Principles mean? And how can you translate them into practice? The important thing to remember is that one must move beyond the strict and narrow view of Lean product development as the full solution. Rather, like the competitive athlete training for the big race, strive for NPD productivity improvement as the goal, and that leads to a broader, more holistic and multi-dimensional view, namely *Lean, Rapid and Profitable New Product Development*. The next four chapters tackle the details of these Seven Principles, complete with illustrations of how they work in practice.

Exhibit 2.7 The Seven Principles of Lean Rapid and Profitable New Product Development

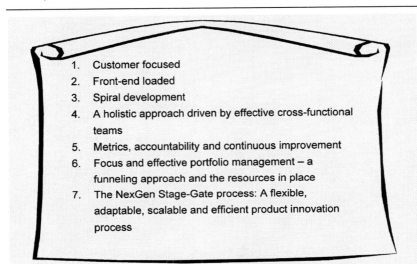

1. Customer focused
2. Front-end loaded
3. Spiral development
4. A holistic approach driven by effective cross-functional teams
5. Metrics, accountability and continuous improvement
6. Focus and effective portfolio management – a funneling approach and the resources in place
7. The NexGen Stage-Gate process: A flexible, adaptable, scalable and efficient product innovation process

Gaining Competitive Product Advantage

Building in the First Three Principles

Introduction

The first three of seven principles of *Lean, Rapid and Profitable New Product Development* deal with gaining a competitive advantage. The first principle is building in a customer-focused strategy. Best performing businesses work hard to understand customer and user needs and customer value. And they use this understanding to develop differentiated, superior products with a compelling value proposition.

The second principle is front-end loading. We explore issues such as doing the right up-front homework, and we deal with how much homework is enough. One goal of front-end work is getting sharp product and project definition. But often things change, so approaches are provided to working with changing customer requirements and potentially flexible product definitions.

The final principle in Chapter 3 is the use of spiral development. This is an effective way of handling the dynamic information process. Spiral development is what fast-paced teams use to get the product right with fluid, changing information and speed to market.

Customer Focused:
Lean, Rapid and Profitable
NPD Principle Number 1

Build a customer focus into your product innovation process! The high-productivity businesses do. Almost 70 percent of best performers have a strong customer focus compared to only 15 percent of poor performers, as shown in Exhibit 3.1. (We use the term "customer" to describe anyone downstream in your value chain; the term "customer" thus includes your immediate customer, their customer, and so on right down to the end user. We do this for convenience, instead of repetitively referring to the "customer and the user").

Customer focus is a critical success driver and a key lean, rapid and profitable principle. The first pay-off is simple. The quest for the differentiated, superior product must begin with a strong customer focus – a thorough understanding of the customers' unmet and unarticulated needs: What is value to the customer? What is a benefit? And what is product quality? With a strong customer focus, the odds of conceiving and developing a winning and more profitable product are much higher. A second pay-off is less obvious. A customer focus reduces time to market. Instead of adding time to the project, a customer focus helps to sharpen the product definition, get the specifications right, and confirm product design early in the process. This effort thus minimizes last minute changes and panics as the product is rolling into launch, where the costs and time to make changes can be huge.

Competitive advantage gained from superior products

The number one key to success in product innovation is developing and delivering differentiated products that offer the customer unique benefits, solve major customer problems, and feature a compelling *value proposition*

**Exhibit 3.1 High-Productivity Businesses Practice the First Principle —
A Customer Focused Product Innovation Effort**

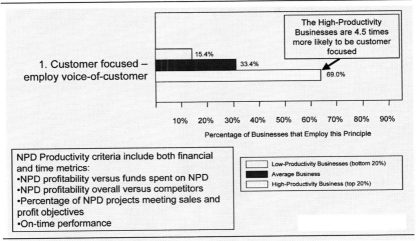

1. Customer focused –
employ voice-of-customer

15.4%

33.4%

69.0%

The High-Productivity
Businesses are 4.5 times
more likely to be customer
focused

10% 20% 30% 40% 50% 60% 70% 80% 90%

Percentage of Businesses that Employ this Principle

NPD Productivity criteria include both financial
and time metrics:
•NPD profitability versus funds spent on NPD
•NPD profitability overall versus competitors
•Percentage of NPD projects meeting sales and
profit objectives
•On-time performance

☐ Low-Productivity Businesses (bottom 20%)
■ Average Business
☐ High-Productivity Business (top 20%)

Source: CEK study, endnote 2.

for the customer or user. Competitive advantage gained from a superior product is the *strongest single driver of profitability* at the project level, yet it is often missed by project teams.[1]

Note: We define a "product" to be *any deliverable to the marketplace* that will generate revenue. This includes a physical product, a service product, or an extended product – a combination of physical product and related bundle of services. Often it is the latter – the extended product – where the source of competitive advantage lies.

High-productivity businesses build this critical success driver, product superiority, into their new products as shown in Exhibit 3.2.[2] Products developed by best performing companies offer customers *benefits that are important* to them. And their products provide the customer *new and unique benefits* – benefits not available on competitive products. This last element truly separates the best from worst performers. Eight times as many best performers develop such unique-benefits products when compared to poor performers!

Best performers' products also offer the customer *superior value* – a better value proposition – again by a wide margin. And their products are also superior to competing products in terms of *meeting customer needs.* Finally, best performers' products are *superior quality* versus competitors, however the customer gauges product quality.

All five elements of competitive advantage gained from a superior product are shown in Exhibit 3.2. What is notable is how strongly the high-productivity businesses manage to build in each element, and how almost all the poor performing businesses seem to miss the mark on these five elements.

Must be customer focused

Conceiving unique, superior products – the number one driver of profitability – is no easy task, however. Review each of the elements in Exhibit 3.2 and consider what work underlies achieving each one. To deliver unique benefits, the developer must understand *what is a benefit* to the customer. Often assumptions about desired features and performance are opinion-based, and turn out not to lead to any benefits at all. The acid test is: Will the customer pay for it? A second key to product advantage is better value for the customer, which is more than simply low price; it means having a good *knowledge of the customer's application* for the product and what improved performance would be worth in use – a *value-in-use analysis.* Meeting customer needs better than competitors' products presumes that the developer also has a solid *understanding of customer needs* (often customers cannot articulate their needs, or do not even know what they need), and also how competitors are falling short. Finally, offering higher quality products means that the developer must have insights into *how the customer gauges quality,* which is often different than how the developer's own Quality Assurance department measures quality.

Exhibit 3.2 Gaining Competitive Advantage Through Product Superiority

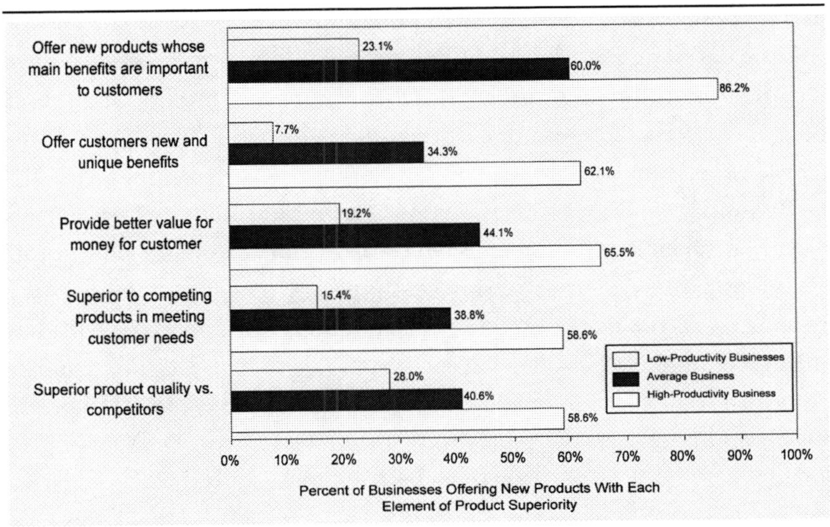

Offer new products whose main benefits are important to customers: 23.1%, 60.0%, 86.2%

Offer customers new and unique benefits: 7.7%, 34.3%, 62.1%

Provide better value for money for customer: 19.2%, 44.1%, 65.5%

Superior to competing products in meeting customer needs: 15.4%, 38.8%, 58.6%

Superior product quality vs. competitors: 28.0%, 40.6%, 58.6%

Legend: Low-Productivity Businesses; Average Business; High-Productivity Business

Percent of Businesses Offering New Products With Each Element of Product Superiority

Source: CEK study, endnote 2.

What a customer focus means

Winning in the marketplace means that your business and project teams must build in a customer-focused strategy, identifying and exploiting competitive advantage. We have five important messages here:

1. Build in key market-focused actions

What work is required in order to become truly customer focused? Our best practices studies provide many insights, with Exhibit 3.3 revealing what the high-productivity businesses do differently from other firms.[3] Let's learn from them.

First, best performers work with innovative or lead customers to generate new product ideas. The theory here is that your customer has your next breakthrough idea; but if you work with average users, you will get average ideas. So identify your *lead customers* – those that are ahead of the wave and particularly innovative – and work closely with them on ideation.[4] Five times as many best performers do this versus poor performers.

Next, work closely with customers to identify their needs and problems before charging into a development program. That is, once you are into a specific development project, build in a good dose of voice-of-customer research (more on how to do this below). Four times as many best performers work closely with customers to identify their needs and problems, as shown in Exhibit 3.3.

Be sure to conduct market research as an input to product design. All too often, when market studies or voice-of-customer work are done, project teams present concepts and solutions to potential customers in order to confirm and validate the concept. Concept testing is good research, but it is not enough. When the concept is internally developed, this assumes your own technical and marketing people already have the solution before they even understand the problem! Voice-of-customer work should be *an input to the design*, not just an after-the-fact check. Sadly, most companies fall far short here: Only a small minority (11 percent) undertake this type of input market research work, but note that a respectable one-third of best performers do.

An example: The pizza brand team at Kraft Foods identified a consumer need for high-quality frozen pizza, closer to restaurant quality. They noted the big gap between the frozen pizza available at the supermarket for $4 and what one could buy at a delivery or take-out pizza shop for $12. Kraft undertook numerous consumer-based quantitative and qualitative tests and identified that the main source of consumer dissatisfaction with frozen pizza was its dry, cardboard-like crust.

Development was initiated in 1995. Improving the crust became the primary challenge for the technical team. Considerable research had been done over the years on the crust, so the technology team was well positioned to develop a higher-quality dough. The team also took advantage of new technologies developed for formula, process, and package, as well as industry research on pre-proofed frozen dough. The result was *rising crust pizza* – a thin crust that rose when in the oven to yield a thicker, less dense and tastier crust. Consumers loved it in taste tests!

Seven years later, *DiGiorno*^{TM} is the number one self-rising pizza brand sold nationally in the U.S. This innovation, based on solid market research to help define the product, refuted the myth that people wouldn't pay a significant premium for a frozen pizza.[5]

Just because the product has entered the development stage is no reason to turn inward. Continue interfacing with the customer all the way through the development stage and beyond. The customer must be an integral part of the development process. Later in this chapter we will see how fast-paced teams use spiral development to achieve this interface via a series of spiral interactions.

Finally, when conducting these various customer investigations, be sure to spend some time on launch issues, gaining insights into the customer's buying behavior – the "who, what, when, where and how" of the purchase decision. With this knowledge, you are better able to craft the market launch plan; for example, your marketing communications, collateral materials, and trade show plans. Pricing is an important facet of your market launch plan; thus, your market research and voice-of-customer work must deal with the issue of quantifying value to the customer – what is the product worth or what is its economic impact on the customer's operations?

2.   Understand unmet needs and customer value

Understanding customer value is fundamental to designing a superior product with a compelling value proposition, and hence is key to success. To understand value, be sure to go beyond what customers say they want – customer wants, requests and specifications. If your project teams come back from field visits with only a list of customer requirements and a specifications list, they have missed the point of the exercise! Instead, focus on the customers' unspoken, unarticulated and often hidden needs.

How does one get at these hidden needs? Recognize that people tend to buy products for one or both of two reasons:

Exhibit 3.3 Customer Focused Means Voice-of-Customer and Market Inputs

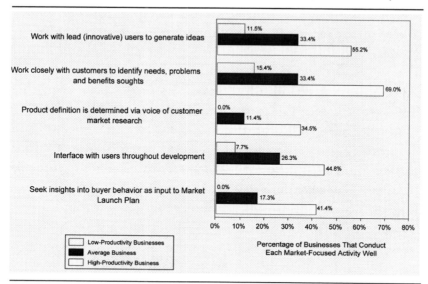

Source: CEK study, endnote 3.

1. *To avoid problems or to solve a problem*: An example is purchasing a Toyota Camry – a solid, conservative automobile with a record of high reliability, a multi-year warranty, and a good local dealer for servicing.

2. *To gain or to seek benefits and values*: An example of this buying behavior is a 50 year-old person purchasing a new and hot convertible sports car.

Both purchase reasons are good sources of customer value. So one approach is to *find big problems…* the bigger the better! And then seek big solutions. A second tactic is to *understand what benefits the user seeks*, and then deliver these major benefits, perhaps in a better or different way.

Needs can thus be discovered by better *understanding the problems* that customers want solved. That is, find the customer's *point of pain* – walk them through their problems and gain an in-depth understanding of these problems. Questions that prove useful, and form the basis of an effective conversation guide for the interview, include:

- What is your current solution (or what product are you buying now)?
- What do you like least about your current product (or solution)... what are your gripes and complaints?
- What is it about this product that causes you to lose sleep... what really annoys you?
- What major problems does this product cause for you? Do you have problems or difficulties when you use this product?

When you ask someone what they are looking for, often they cannot answer; but ask them what is bothering them – their gripes and complaints – and they open up.

An example: A voice-of-customer visit team from Goulds Pumps (a manufacturer of large industrial pumps) uncovered a significant unmet need and major problem faced by customers. Electric power costs are rising and, not surprisingly, all pump users seek higher efficiency pumps. But pump design is quite advanced and further gains in pump efficiency are just about exhausted. When visiting pump users, the visit team noticed that often the pump is operating at 100% capacity, yet only a fraction of the delivered flow is needed. The user's solution was to install a valve and cut back on the flow, analogous to driving an automobile with your foot heavy on the accelerator, and your other foot on the brake to slow the car down. The Goulds solution: the Smart Pump. By building in a series of flow and pressure sensors and some computing capability, the pump senses what flow is needed, and slows down accordingly, thereby saving power and costs. It's been a big winner for Goulds and another example of how voice-of-customer really works even in so-called mature markets!

Needs can also be discovered by focusing on *benefits sought.* That is, uncover the benefits that the product or service features deliver to the customer – for example, what the product lets the customer or user do. Thus, when meeting with customers, be sure to understand:

- what their current solution is (what product they are now buying)
- what it lets them do
- what features, performance or functionality they like most about it
- what these features and performance let them do — why they are important
- what it does not let them do that they would like it to
- what they might want in the way of a new or improved product
- why they mentioned those features and performance — again what they would let them do and why they are important.

These and similar questions form the basis of a conversation or interview guide useful in gaining insights into benefits that customers seek. By involving the core team all team members gain an understanding of what is truly important to the customer and why.

3. The core project team must do the in-the-field work

An understanding of value and unmet needs can only be gained through in-the-field voice-of-customer work. That is, the core project team must work with the customer — face-to-face visits — in order to gain these insights. These visitations or face-to-face research sessions should be undertaken by the project team, working in sub-teams of two to three people. Get the entire project team involved and doing this field research work.

Note that there is a big difference between "voice of the salesperson" and voice of the customer; it is not good enough to rely on a third party, such as a salesperson or product manager to seek customer insights. These people provide good clues, but sometimes these are biased or limited. Rather, the project team must go out and touch real customers and users! And make sure that the technical people on the project team are involved too, not just the sales or marketing person on the team. *Marketing is too important to be left to marketing people!*

4. Begin early

This work must begin early in the project. Voice-of-customer work done earlier is likely to have much more impact than such work done well into the development stage. By then, the important decisions have already been made. Thus, undertake market research as an input to the design, and not just as a confirmation. For example, make sure the voice-of-customer work is done long before the final product definition is decided. But don't stop there. The project team must have constant customer interaction, testing and validation of the product with customers and users as it evolves from concept through to final product.

5. Broaden the base

Broaden the base of these customer and user contacts and visits. Be sure to go beyond the lead and convenient user. Thus, the interviews must be at multiple customer sites. Over-reliance on a single customer may be convenient, but that customer does not speak for the entire market. Note that while the project may have been triggered by a single customer request, it is always prudent to check out other and similar potential customers – maybe they have the same need too, and their input should also be sought. Too many project teams focus on a single customer, when really the project should have and could have been a "market product" with a much greater sales potential. Finally, it may be necessary to move down the value chain, seeking inputs from customers at different levels. Each of these customers may be a key purchase influencer (or a potential blocker) and their inputs should be sought.

Types of information sought

What types of information should be sought by the project team when conducting the market investigations? The types of information that high-productivity businesses seek and get in the early stages of the project – before development begins – provides a clue. As seen in Exhibit 3.4, best performers obtain solid information on:

- customer needs, problems and benefits sought
- the competitive situation: who they are, their products and pricing, and their strengths and weaknesses
- customer reaction to the proposed product concept
- information on customer price sensitivity – a good understanding of customer value
- market size and market potential
- expected sales revenue to be generated by the new product – a projection.[6]

What stands out in Exhibit 3.4 is how much better the quality of market information the high-productivity businesses gather is. Three or four times as many best performers obtain quality market information as do poor performers. This information is strongly linked to positive performance. Use the list of items above and in Exhibit 3.3 as a guide to the types

Exhibit 3.4 Vital Market Information Before Development Begins

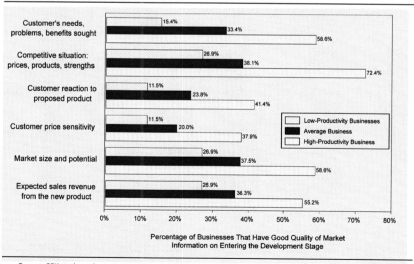

Source: CEK study, endnote 6.

of information your project teams should seek and have before they enter the development stage of a new product project.

Front-End Loaded: Lean, Rapid and Profitable NPD Principle Number 2

Front-end homework is essential

High-productivity businesses front-end load their new product projects – see Exhibit 3.5. That is, they move the centre of gravity of their projects forward, focusing more time, attention and effort on the pre-development stages of their projects than do poor performers.

Many businesses distinguish between light homework, often called scoping or "desk research", and heavy homework, such as building the business case, as shown in Exhibit 3.6. Both of these front-end or home-work stages are vital. It's false economy to cut corners here! They are key

Exhibit 3.5 Front-End Loading Projects — Highly Productive Businesses Practice the Second Principle

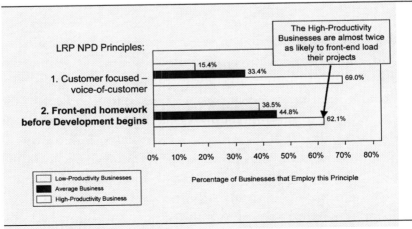

Source: CEK study, endnote 6.

Exhibit 3.6 Front-End Loaded — LRP NPD Principle Number 2

✓ Focus on the front-end of the project
✓ The two homework stages (Stage 1 and Stage 2) are critical to success
✓ Purpose of front-end work here:
   - defines the product and project
   - provides information vital to the Go/Kill investment decision

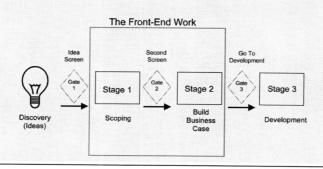

to both timeliness (on-time performance and time efficiency) and profitability.[7]

High-productivity businesses do a superlative job in these early stages of projects.[8] They understand and practice the principle of front-end loading. Consistently, as Exhibit 3.7 reveals, best performers do much better job on the front-end work, proficiently undertaking seven key activities:

1. Preliminary market assessment: A quick assessment of the market to determine market size and potential, customer interest, initial insights into customer needs, requirements and value, and the competitive situation.

2. Technical assessment: A pre-development assessment of the technical challenge, identifying the probable technical solution (on paper), the development route, technical challenges, risks and potential showstoppers, the IP situation, and outside technology required (including the need for technology alliances). This is the best executed activity in the front-end, with almost half of businesses rated well here.

3. Source-of-supply assessment: An initial appraisal of source of product supply, including operation requirements, probable materials and

equipment needs, and possible outsourcing needs – suppliers and partners or alliances. This is judged to be a very weak area, with about one business in five doing a solid job. Too often, project teams do not involve the manufacturing or operations people early enough in the project, when key decisions – such as product design decisions – are taken that later impact strongly on the operations people.

4. Market research: A more in-depth market investigation, involving the project team doing voice-of-customer research, as highlighted above. Market size and segmentation analysis may be conducted here as well. This is also a very weak area, with only 18 percent of businesses judged to do this well; but, again, best performers seem to do better here, by an almost five-to-one ratio versus poor performers.

5. Concept testing: This is a different type of customer input, where the proposed product, perhaps as a model, concept or virtual prototype, is presented to customers, and feedback is sought. Interest, liking and purchase intent are established. This is good and necessary research, but it is no substitute for the voice-of-customer work as input outlined above.

6. Value-to-the-customer assessment: This is a value-in-use analysis, whereby the product's value is quantified. This activity usually involves looking at the economic impact on customers' operations versus how they solve their problem now (for example, versus competitive solutions and then considering competitive prices and their products' cost in use). This is perhaps the weakest of the front-end activities with only one in six businesses doing this well. Again best performers handle this value assessment much better – by a nine-to-one ratio. Still this is a task needing improvement for many businesses.

7. Business and financial analysis: Integrating the data obtained in the homework stages into a business case, which features a full financial and business analysis including a sensitivity analysis.

Build these seven key actions into your front-end! Use the activity list above and in Exhibit 3.7 as a guide, and ensure that these homework activities are executed well and are a way of doing business for your

Exhibit 3.7 Front-End Homework is Essential

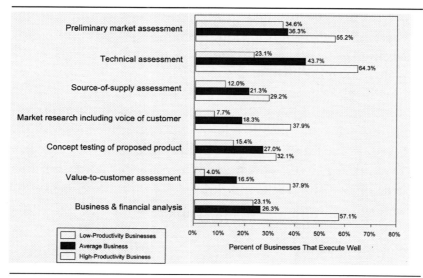

Source: CEK study, endnote 8.

significant new product projects. They are important actions, are what front-loaded means, and are executed well in businesses achieving lean yet profitable innovation.

> *An example:* Procter & Gamble relies on their SIMPL idea-to-launch model to drive new products to market, which requires project teams to do their homework early in the project.[9] For example, in P&G's Cosmetics business, much consumer research work was done and consumer insights gained that led to winning new product concepts. One resulting big success is *Outlast*[TM] *by Cover Girl.* This 10 hour lipstick – a kiss-proof, long-lasting lipstick – uses a unique two-part application system (first a color and then a gloss) to produce an enduring lip color. A second winner – *Lipfinity*[TM] *by Max Factor* – was also introduced, again using the SIMPL idea-to-launch framework and based on heavy front-end homework. Both new products have been huge successes not only in the United States, but around the world, and are testimony to the pay-offs from solid front-end homework.

Does more front-end homework mean longer times to market?

Many senior managers and project teams think they can save a few months by cutting out the front-end work in projects, in effect circumventing the homework stages. "Why go through all these activities" (listed above), they ask, "when a few well-based assumptions and guesses will do?" These teams are in such a big hurry that they move an ill-defined, ill-researched project into development, hoping to drive it to market quickly.

Sadly, the overwhelming evidence suggests that they usually get into problems later on, as everything starts to go wrong: Some of the guesses, opinions and assumptions were very much in error. And so these project teams end up taking far more extra time than the time they saved at the beginning. Here are the facts:

- More time and money spent on the front-end greatly improves the odds of success – there is clear evidence for this! New product projects with solid front-end homework have more than double the success rates and double the market share than those projects that lacked good homework.[10]
- Next, more and better front-end work results in better and sharper product and project definition, which then speeds up the development and testing stages, with less recycling and wasted time. Note that solid front-end work is the number two driver of on-time performance.[11]
- Finally, front-end homework done well anticipates product problems and design changes. These product design changes are made early in the game, rather than as the product is going to market.

Build in a product definition step before development begins

The product definition establishes the goal-posts for the project team – what's expected – so that the physical development effort can speed towards its goal. These goal-posts must be established before development begins, and so part of the front-end work is *defining the product*. This is an all-party agreement between team members and senior management. And this is a vital facet of the front-end loading, as shown in Exhibit 3.8.[12] Note that, before development begins, high-productivity businesses delineate the target market clearly; they also define the product concept – what the product will be and do, the benefits the product will deliver to the customer, and the positioning strategy (including target price point). Many of these items are poorly handled by the typical company, and are dismally executed by poor performers. Best performers also nail down the product requirements, features and specifications, something that most businesses seem to do reasonably well.

Many firms have a product definition template built into their product innovation process and its business case. A good outline of such a template is shown in Exhibit 3.9, with eight key items included.[13]

Unstable product specifications and project scope creep are two of the greatest time wasters in product development. In the case of scope creep, the project may begin as a simple one – perhaps a single customer request for a minor modification – but grows over time to be a much larger project with many potential customers. The second time waster, unstable product specifications, is the situation that occurs when the project team believes they have defined the product specs and charges into the development stage. But then things start to change. New information becomes available, and the specifications and requirements start to shift. The team finds it is in the unenviable position of chasing moving goalposts. And it is very difficult to score a goal, with much recycling back into development to handle yet one more design change request, but very late in the project.

Note that much of this "new information" that arrives at the eleventh hour is usually not that new at all. It was readily available had anyone bothered to make the effort to obtain it. Thus, last minute changes to the product and its specs are most often the result of poor and inadequate front-end work.

High-productivity businesses strive for and get *stable product definition early* and much more often than do poor performers, as seen in Exhibit 3.8. Perfect stability is never guaranteed of course, as some things always change. This is unavoidable. But when *everything changes*, as is so often the case, this situation is unacceptable. Best performers manage to achieve reasonably stable product definitions because they front-end load their projects – they get the facts up front: for example, inputs from their extensive voice-of-customer work and competitive analysis. Then they base their

Exhibit 3.8 Product Definition — Key to NPD Productivity

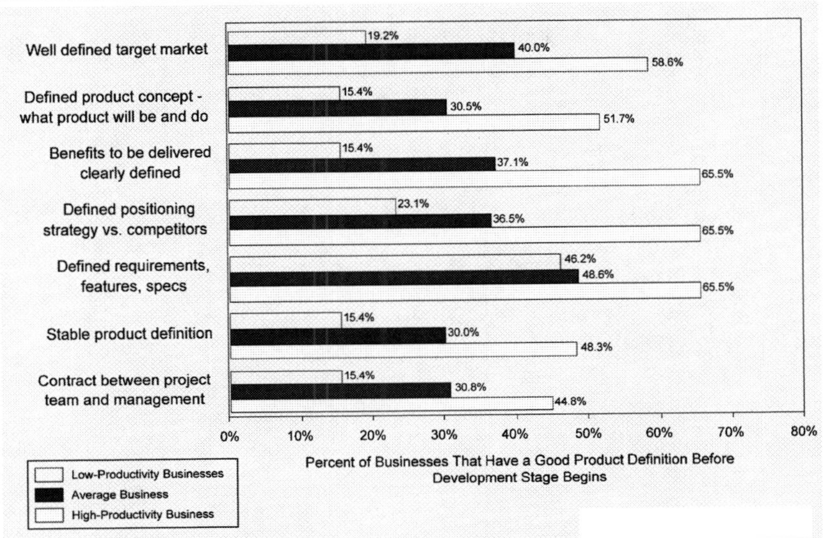

Source: CEK study, endnote 12.

product definition on these facts rather than on hearsay and opinion.

The concept of *teaming contracts* between the project team and senior management is relatively new but is seen in some businesses, particularly in better performing ones. The teaming contract is simply a pseudo contract between the project team undertaking the project and the senior management gatekeeping team that accepts the business case and approves the project for development. This contract specifies what the project team will deliver (a developed product according to the product definition, for example) and when. It defines what management's obligations are; for example, resource commitments of people and money to the project team. This contract is signed by all the team members and senior management, and is yet another tool for locking in the product definition.

How much front-end work is enough?

Project teams face two difficult issues here. The first is how to go about doing the right front-end homework, and how much information is enough. The second is working with fluid information; for example,

Exhibit 3.9 The Integrated Product Definition

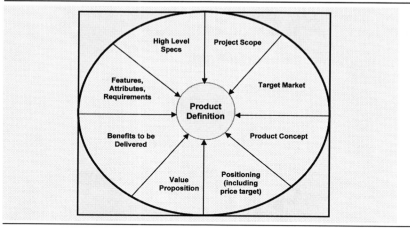

Source: Stage-Gate Inc. www.stage-gate.com

changing customer requirements and shifting market conditions. Fluid information often leads to fluid and unstable flexible product definitions.

The great majority of high-productivity businesses handle both issues well, in marked contrast to poor performing businesses. The fundamental principle is this: Undertake only enough homework to yield data that is essential for the key decisions you must make. Examples of key decisions in these earlier stages are design decisions (the product definition) and Go/Kill decisions on the project. The rule is simple: It's alright to move forward without complete information. That is, the project team can begin the next activity within a stage with partial information.

Moving forward with partial information is the principle of *simultaneous execution*. An example is Toyota.[14] Here, development teams are encouraged to do the most they can with only that portion of the design data that is not likely to change. But Toyota management is quick to point out that working with early and unstable data will result in excessive waste, and probably require a longer duration than the original linear process. Thus at Toyota, each function's processes are designed to move forward simultaneously, building on stable data as it becomes available. The key to making simultaneous execution work is to be careful not to use unstable or unreliable information to make key decisions.

Dealing with fluid information

A useful chart to help project teams think through the dilemma of how much information is enough is shown in Exhibit 3.10. By the time the project team believes they are nearing the end of their front-end work, they should have gathered much information on the project:

- Some information is fact-based; for example, user problems that the team identifies in their voice-of-customer study, or certain features and performance characteristics confirmed by customers in a concept test. Other information is largely opinion, hearsay and speculation; for example, a salesperson's belief about what the winning product should be.
- Some information is fairly stable and not likely to change; for example, the estimated size of the market or the size of specific customer segments in the market, or certain product performance requirements confirmed with the customer. Other information is much more dynamic and fluid, such as pricing information from the marketplace, and certain customer requirements for product features and functionality that the customer acknowledges are "yet to be determined".

The two-by-two matrix in Exhibit 3.10 captures both dimensions: fluid versus fixed information, and fact-based versus opinion-based information. Project teams should sort their information into the four quadrants and, in so doing, better understand what information they can use to base their decisions on. Clearly, information that falls in the lower right quadrant – opinion information that is also highly changeable – is the worst information, and basing key decisions, such as the product definition, on this type of information is folly. Rather, adhering to the principle of simultaneous execution, the project team should only use information in the upper left quadrant to base their decisions on. In some cases, this quadrant exercise in Exhibit 3.10 suggests that the team has not yet done enough homework; in other cases, the exercise results in a decision to move forward using available information.

Exhibit 3.10 Use Stable and Reliable Information Only For Key Decisions

	Information Stability	
	Fixed	**Fluid**
Fact-Based	Stable and reliable information: Base your key decisions on information here, e.g., Design, Go/Kill	Unstable information: Do not use for key decisions. Build steps in to get constantly updated data
Opinion-Based	Can base early decisions (Go/Kill; preliminary Product Definition) on this information. Undertake studies to get facts	Poor and unstable information: Do not base decisions on this

(left axis label: Information Reliability)

Fixed versus fluid product definitions

What this means is that, for some projects, the product definition may be partially fixed and partially fluid on entering the development stage. The project team must specify what elements of the definition are based on facts that are stable versus facts that may change over time – what is fixed and what is fluid in the product definition must be clearly noted. The expectation is that at least 70 percent of the product definition should be fixed; that is, fact-based and stable. If not, there is not much of a product definition in place, a signal that more homework needs to be done! If part of the product definition remains unstable (perhaps 30 percent), then steps such as spirals must be laid out for the next stages of the project that are designed to nail down that portion or 30 percent of the product definition that remains fluid.

Spiral Development:
Lean, Rapid and Profitable
NPD Principle Number 3

Spiral development is the way fast-paced teams handle the dynamic information process with fluid, changing information. Spiral development helps the team get the product and the product definition right, in spite of the fact that some information is fluid and some may even be unreliable when the team moves into the development stage. (Note: The high-productivity businesses are more than five times as likely to employ spiral development than low-productivity businesses. See Exhibit 3.11)

Many businesses use what we call a *rigid and linear process* for product innovation. This is wrong! An example is sketched in Exhibit 3.12. The project team diligently visits customers in the pre-development or front-end stages and determines customer needs and requirements as best they can. Front-end work or homework is properly done, and the product specs are determined. The product definition is fixed, perhaps even using a template as in Exhibit 3.9. So far, so good.

The development stage (shown as Stage 3 in Exhibit 3.12) gets underway, but proceeds in *a linear and rigid fashion*. The project team hunkers down and moves the project forward following a heads-down, rather than a heads-up approach – much like a farmer dutifully following his plow, oblivious to what's going on around him. For outsiders, it's as though the project has moved into a black box called "development" – or is it a black hole? Some 10 or 15 months pass, and at the end of this linear development stage, the product is developed and is ready for field trials or customer tests.

Then everything goes wrong. When presented with the prototype product for testing, the original customers, contacted 10 or 15 months earlier, now indicate that "this is not quite what we had in mind" or that "things have changed over the last while". Or perhaps a new competitive product has been launched that alters the competitive landscape.

Exhibit 3.11 Spiral Development — Highly Productive Businesses Practice the Third Principle

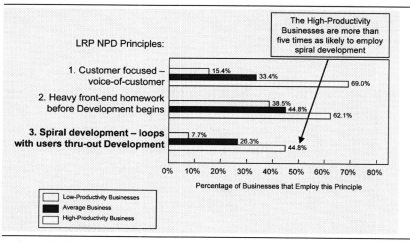

Source: CEK study, endnote 12.

Exhibit 3.12 The Rigid Linear Product Innovation Process Does Not Work

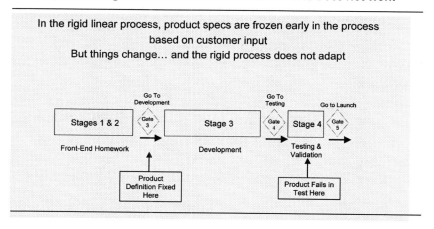

The point is that, by proceeding in a relative information vacuum in a linear and rigid process, the team set themselves up for failure. Maybe they did not get the initial product requirements 100 percent right – maybe they missed some key points when they did their initial customer visitation work, or maybe they misinterpreted some customer requirements. Or perhaps things really did change in the 10 to 15 months that ensued. And now the team is faced with back-tracking into the development stage for another attempt at the product… another victim of a rigid, linear process that does not adapt to changing circumstances.

Things always seem to change during the course of a project, the result of fluid or sometimes even unreliable information. Even with the best front-end work, things still change, albeit far less so. For example:

- the product definition is not quite right in the first place
- market and customer requirements change
- a new competitive product is introduced
- new technical possibilities or solutions become available

The point is that a rigid and linear process does not work because it is not adaptive and does not respond to changing and fluid information.

Build in the spirals

Smart project teams and businesses practice spiral development. They use a series of iterative steps or "loops" whereby successive versions of the product are shown to the customer to seek feedback and verification, as shown in Exhibit 3.13. These loops are a series of "build-test-feedback-and-revise" iterations, and their shape leads to the term "spiral development".

The spiral principle is based on the fact that customers do not really know what they looking for until they see it or experience it. So get something in front of the customer – anything, even if it's still a long way from the final product – and start early. And then seek fast and confirmatory feedback, making the necessary changes to the product and getting an even closer version in front of the customer for the next iteration. But words of warning: Don't fully develop the product and start presenting real prototypes early in the process. The notion here is to get something in front of the customer initially that you can put together quickly and inexpensively.

The spirals in practice

How does spiral development work in practice? A sample set of spirals is shown in Exhibit 3.13. Note that these loops or spirals are built in from the front-end stages through the development stage and into the testing stage.

The first loop or spiral is the voice-of-customer study – a user needs and want study – where project team members visit customers to better understand their unmet needs, problems and benefits sought in the new product. At this point, the team probably has very little to show the customer, and that is the way it should be. The purpose of this visit is to listen and watch, not to "show and tell".

The second spiral, which is labeled a full proposition concept test in Exhibit 3.13, is where the project team presents *a representation of the proposed product*. Note that the product and project have still not yet entered the development stage, so there is no real product available. Depending on the type of product and industry, this representation can be:

- a computer-generated virtual prototype; for example, in the case of engineering products, electronics products, or even jewelry
- a hand-made model, for example, in the case of furniture, building materials or even computer chips
- a crude protocept, in the case of food products or consumer non-durables
- or even a few computer screens for new software or a new lab instrument.

The product obviously does not work at this early stage, and, in some presentations, is only two-dimensional. But it is enough to give the customer a "feel" for what the product will be and do. The product presentation should be accompanied by simulated collaterals or selling materials: a dummy brochure, a simulated spec sheet, a sales presentation on PowerPoint, or even a storyboard with sound track to simulate a television ad. At the end of the presentation, and following the question period, the customer is asked the standard concept test questions:

- Are you interested?
- Did you like it? What do you like best? Like least?
- Did you like it better than your current product or solution? Why or why not?
- What would you expect to pay (relative to what you are now paying)?
- Would you buy?

Feedback is sought on dislikes and changes required, and the project team moves to finalize their product definition as part of the Stage 2 business case in Exhibit 3.13.

Exhibit 3.13 Spiral Development — A Series of "Build-Test-Feedback and Revise" Iterations, Loops or Spirals

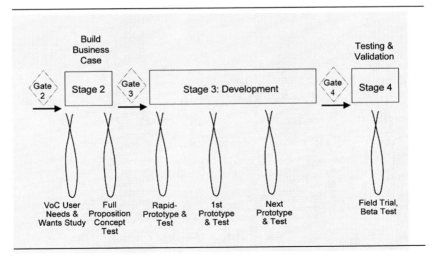

Moving into the development stage in Exhibit 3.13, within weeks the team produces the next and more complete version of the product, perhaps a crude model or a rapid prototype. They test this with customers, using much the same methodology as above and again seek feedback, which they use to rapidly revise and build the first working prototype... and so on, with each successive version of the product getting closer and closer to the final product, and at the same time, closer and closer to the customer's ideal. Fortunately, over the past few years, better technology has appeared on the market to make this much easier to do. So be sure to use the available tools when developing successive versions of the product.

Remember: Get something in front of customers early and often, because people don't know what they're looking for until they see it! So be creative when developing this series of successive presentations of the product, but without spending huge amounts of money. The goal here is to get a product definition and get it quickly in spite of fluid market conditions, but without developing the full or real product until the very end.

An example: A hi-tech valve manufacturer consistently seemed to get into trouble as its projects neared commercialization. An in-depth assessment of the business' development process revealed the problem: a rigid, linear process that did not adapt to changing information.

Traditionally, the technical and marketing people in the firm would visit pharmaceutical users (their target customers) to determine a set of requirements for the next new-and-improved valve. And the team usually got the product definition right. So far, so good. Then the project moved into development for about 12 months, after which the new product was ready for field trials. And that's where everything went wrong. During the course of the 12 months, things had indeed changed, and the buyers had somehow lost their appetite for the new product, or the product wasn't quite right.

The company has since implemented spiral development. Visit teams still undertake voice-of-customer research and determine product requirements, much as they did before. But early in the project, even before development begins, *virtual prototypes* are shown to the customer: These are computer generated simulated three dimensional drawings of the proposed new product on a video screen, which the customer sees and provides feedback on.

Once the project is released for Development, within weeks a wax model of the valve is created and shared with the customer. True, the customer cannot install or use the new valve, but he can pick it up, inspect it, and provide comment. Next a *rapid prototype* is generated – a plastic model created via stereographic lithography direct from CAD software. This version is even closer to the final product, so the customer is able to provide even more informed feedback and comment. Thus the project proceeds through Development and into field trails, relying on these rapid spirals to finalize the product's design, but most importantly, to get it right!

Some cautions with spiral development

An important challenge that most project teams face when using the spiral development approach is how to deal with intellectual property. First, before any spirals or customer visitation takes place at all, it is essential that the project team seeks and gets legal advice on intellectual property issues. Even the initial voice-of-customer studies can be problematic, for example: If a customer makes a suggestion, who "owns" the idea or suggestion?

A second and related issue is the possibility that competitors will find out about the product very early. Although you probably trust your customers, there are some who may be less than discreet and transfer information that you shared with them to a competitor. A non-disclosure agreement helps, but is not a 100 percent deterrent, as most businesses are loathe to take legal action against a talkative customer. The best bet here is to share or show only those facets of the product that really are not highly confidential. For example, if you are developing a new electronic instrument, show the customer what it looks like, how it interfaces with the user, what the screens and displays look like, but not the details of how it works. In short, show the customer the outside but not the inside of the box! And don't leave written or electronic information behind that a customer could pass on to others. So, even if the customer does talk to a competitor, without materials describing what the product is or does, and without an understanding of how it works, there really is not much information of consequence that they can pass on. A final tactic is to present multiple concepts or protocepts as long as these are easy and cheap to develop. Only one is the real concept, but it is sufficiently disguised among the rest so that little damage is done if the information is leaked to competitors.

One danger of early spirals is that the customer misconstrues the concept or rapid prototype presentation for *a real product*. That is, they demand that the product be made available to them right away! Sometimes this is the result of poor communication: The project team did not make it clear to the customer that this was a concept test or rapid prototype test only... not an offer to sell. We often draw the analogy between a concept car at an automotive show versus a production car. Put in those terms, most people understand the difference. Another tip: If there are salespeople on the project team, don't let them make the concept presentation, and especially prevent them from making promises to the customer about when and where the new concept-product will be available. Very quickly, the meeting turns into a sales presentation rather than a concept or rapid prototype test. And then you are faced with dealing with oral commitments that you cannot keep.

An effective way to handle unstable and fluid information

Spiral development works and works well! True, there are a few issues and concerns with spiral development, such as intellectual property, confidentiality, and showing one's hand early. Astute project teams take action on these. But on balance, spiral development is an excellent principle and should be built into your product innovation process. These loops or spirals enable teams to move quickly to confirm elements of the product's definition and design. The iterations with users separate facts from speculation, and they establish interest, liking and purchase intent. And if customer requirements or market conditions change, these loops allow the project team to respond quickly. By way of these spirals, the team moves rapidly to a finalized and winning new product.

Conclusion

You have seen the first three principles of Lean, *Rapid and Profitable NPD* – they are summarized in Exhibit 3.14. All three principles deal with how to gain competitive advantage by developing a superior and differentiated product, one that truly delights the customer. The principle of being customer focused is fundamental to understanding the customer needs and what they value. High-productivity businesses embrace this principle. Front-end loading projects is the second principle, again practiced by best performers. Here the goal is to get the facts so that key decisions, such as the product definition and the Go-to-Development decisions, are better ones. Finally, the principle of spiral development enables project teams to move quickly to a confirmed and winning product definition and design, while at the same time dealing with unstable information. Implement these first three principles, and watch your results improve. But there are another three principles to come in the next chapter, so read on!

Exhibit 3.14 Summary — The Seven Principles of LRP NPD

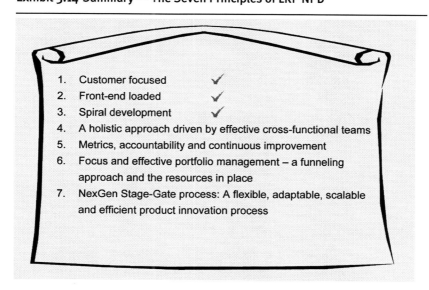

1. Customer focused ✓
2. Front-end loaded ✓
3. Spiral development ✓
4. A holistic approach driven by effective cross-functional teams
5. Metrics, accountability and continuous improvement
6. Focus and effective portfolio management – a funneling approach and the resources in place
7. NexGen Stage-Gate process: A flexible, adaptable, scalable and efficient product innovation process

CHAPTER 4

Driving the New Product Project to Market

Building in the Next Two Principles

Driving the new product project to market quickly but effectively is the goal of the next two principles of *Lean, Rapid and Profitable (LRP) new product development.* Principle Number 4 is adopting a *holistic approach* to product innovation driven by *effective cross-functional teams* – teams built for speed to market. Best performers treat product innovation as a holistic endeavor, involving all functions of the business, with all departments and functions working together to deliver the winning product. A cross-functional team is at the heart of this holistic approach, so best performers work hard at making a team approach and team culture work. In this chapter we reveal some of the best practices that help make teams more effective in product innovation.

The fifth principle is difficult to implement, and very much part of the lean manufacturing culture: installing performance metrics, holding teams accountable for delivering results against these metrics, and then applying continuous learning and improvement so that errors and deficiencies are corrected. This principle is the second major topic of this chapter.

A Holistic Approach Driven By Effective Cross-Functional Teams: Lean, Rapid and Profitable NPD Principle Number 4

A well-run new product project is much like a small business start up. The project team is the start-up group, lead by a champion or captain. The team and captain are very entrepreneurial, and move diligently and quickly to their goal, namely to get a winning product on the market. The team requires the talents of many different types of people to be success-ful: technical experts, marketers, salespeople, operations people and others such as finance, legal, regulatory and purchasing. So the project or "start up business" is very much a holistic enterprise, involving all departments: It is a *business* project and not just an R&D or marketing project.

The project or start-up business has investors or angels – we call these the "gatekeepers" in a business. They are the people who own the resources required by the project leader and team to move their project forward. They meet the project team at gate meetings to review progress and to make the next commitment of resources, much like an investor group would.

The model of an entrepreneurial business start-up is a good analogy and model to apply for major new product projects in your business. The basic elements of your product innovation system (people, processes and technology) must be fully integrated, aligned and designed to be mutually supportive.[1] And highly skilled, intelligently organized people – the proj-ect team and the gatekeepers – are the heart of this product development system, with all functions within the organization aligned to the process and to the project.

A *true* cross-functional team

Product innovation is very much a team activity. Therefore it is crucial that you organize your product innovation effort and projects around a *true* cross-functional team approach. High-productivity businesses understand the message (see Exhibit 4.1). They overwhelmingly embrace the principle of a holistic approach driven by true cross functional teams, with three-quarters of best performers adopting this approach – twice as many as poor performers.[2]

An effective cross-functional team approach is also the strongest driver of cycle time reduction by far! The correlation data in Exhibit 4.2 show how strongly different drivers are connected both to time metrics (time efficiency and on-time performance) as well as to project profitability. These data are from a specific study that focused on drivers of successful new product projects.[3] Note the dominant result of having an effective cross-functional team in place: It is the number one driver of project time, and the number five driver of project profits. Tom Peters makes an even stronger case, arguing that 75 percent of time slippage is due to siloing (sending memos up and down a vertical organizational structure) and sequential problem solving (each function doing its own part of the project, and then handing it off to the next functional department, much like a relay race).[4] Functional silos thwart effective communication among team players from different departments, and are the antithesis of a holistic approach. And sequential problem solving – the relay race or series approach – adds much time to projects and also detracts from project accountability.

A clearly defined core team of responsible experts

A truly cross-functional team is one that is comprised of members from different functions in your business: marketing, engineering or R&D, sales, operations and, perhaps, finance and purchasing. Most businesses embrace this approach, as shown in Exhibit 4.3, with almost 80 percent of best performers consistent here.[5] Where high-productivity businesses

Exhibit 4.1 Highly Productive Businesses Practice The 4th Principle — A Holistic Approach Driven by Effective Cross-Functional Teams

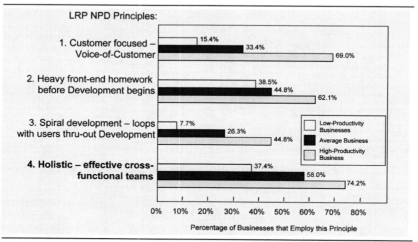

Source: CEK study, endnote 2.

Exhibit 4.2 Impact of Factors on Project Time and Profit

Correlation to Time and Profit		
Factor	With Time Efficiency & On-Time Launch	With Profitab ility (NPV, Payback)
Holistic: cross -functional teams	0.483	0.351
Front-end loaded	0.408	0.366
Customer focused	0.406	0.440 2
Sharp, early product definition	0.242	0.413 3
Market attractiveness	0.215	0.312
Quality of the Launch	0.205	0.286
Unique, superior product	no effect	0.530 1

Correlation: a 0-1 measure; 1.0 means perfect 1:1 correlation

Source: Cooper & Kleinschmidt, endnote 3

really stand out is that team members are *clearly defined*. On exiting each Go/Kill gate, it is clear who is on the *core team* and, therefore, who is accountable for the end result, versus who is just a resource person to the team. (Resource people are "peripheral players"; they attend some team meetings, provide some help, but are not on the core team and are not accountable for the ultimate success and failure of the project; nor do they share the reward in the event of a winner). By contrast, a minority of low-productivity businesses clearly define who the core team is on exiting each gate – a small point it seems, but critical when it comes to Principle Number 5 (later in this chapter), metrics and accountability.

Another important characteristic of a true cross-functional team is that each team member has *an equal stake in and commitment to* the project. Just like that football or soccer team you might have played on in high school, every team member has but one goal – winning the game by launching a winning new product. Team members are not on the team as functional representatives, nor as spokespeople for their respective function. They leave their functional clothing behind them when they join this team.

In best practice companies, product innovation teams are increasingly teams of *responsible experts* – much like the business start-up group – who *focus on the result* rather than on the procedure. At Procter & Gamble, for example, a major behavioral shift occurred when management demanded that team members redirect attention and effort to "winning in the marketplace" and away from simply "getting one's project approved" or "preparing the necessary paperwork for the next gate meeting."[6] Procedure is important, but only to the extent that it improves the odds of achieving the desired end result. Thus, the effective product innovation team is much like a surgical team: It ensures that the patient lives, as well as having a successful operation. And like a surgical team or business start-up team, teams think for themselves. They map out their path forward, and propose the plans and solutions, rather than being ordered or led by their bosses.

The entire project, end-to-end

In effective product innovation teams, every team member is responsible for the *entire project*, not just each person's "little piece" of the project. The team sinks or swims together! This also means that they are responsible for more than *just one phase* or stage of the project – they do not come on the field, play a few plays, and then leave the field for good. This *end to end team* is an important facet of the way best performers play the game. Note from Exhibit 4.3 that high-productivity businesses rely on end-to-end teams by a three-to-one ratio when compared to poorly performing businesses.

By contrast, poorer performers tend to change the team dramatically as the project moves from stage to stage. In some businesses, the entire project team leaves the field and the project is handed off to the "commercial people" for the final stage or two of the project. The argument here is that the skill set is different, so change the entire team. True, some new skills may be required as one shifts from the development stage to testing and, finally, to launch. But keep the team together as much as possible, adding some players – from operations and the salesforce – as the project nears commercialization. But the core team remains intact! That's what high-productivity businesses do.

By constantly changing the team, and by not embracing this end-to-end team philosophy, you lose four important assets:

- *Momentum* – every time there is a major change in team members or, worse yet a hand-off, the project loses momentum and it loses time.
- *Passion* – motivated and well-led team members build up passion for their project. Every time you change the team composition, you lose some passionate players and passion for the project.
- *Knowledge* – when teams change partway through the project, the key knowledge holders leave the field; often it takes a long time for the new team additions to gain the same knowledge, if at all.
- *Accountability* – every time you change the team, accountability disappears. The new team members can conveniently blame the previous team for all the mistakes or if targets are missed.

So if you are content to give up these four assets – momentum, passion, knowledge and accountability – keep changing the team and its players. That's what poor performers do!

The team leader as lead entrepreneur

Effective cross-functional teams have a *clearly defined team leader*, as shown in Exhibit 4.3. Surprisingly, in half of low-productivity businesses, it is not clear even who the project team captain is! This leader is usually designated fairly early in the life of a project, shortly after the idea has been screened. The team leader is the captain of the team or champion of the project, and is most definitely an active player on the field, much like the captain of a football or soccer team (as opposed to being a cheerleader or coach-manager on the side of the field).

The product innovation project leader is very much an *entrepreneur-leader* and not an administrator. The leader acts like the founder of a new business start-up. He or she helps the team understand their mission and, then, working with the project team, defines the team's targets, all the while seeking inputs from multiple sources. The leader is also the person who communicates this vision and targets to senior management, the gatekeepers.

The team leader remains *leader from end-to-end*, a practice endorsed by high-productivity businesses two-to-one versus poor performing businesses, as shown in Exhibit 4.3. In the case of very long projects, sometimes the team leader needs to be relieved for awhile (or a new skill set is required). In this case, appoint an "assistant captain" who, much like the pilot and co-pilot arrangement in an aircraft cockpit, takes over the controls for awhile. But neither the captain nor co-pilot get off the plane. Both remain on the project until the end.

Additionally, on very large projects, some best practice companies assign a *project manager* to the project to lend support to the team leader. The project manager is an administrative person, often seconded from the project management office (PMO). His or her job is to handle the project management tasks: developing and updating timelines; handling

Exhibit 4.3 Organize Project Teams for Maximum Productivity

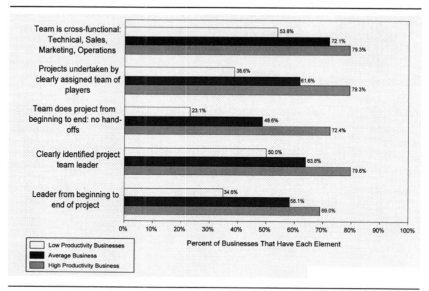

Source: CEK study, endnote 5.

the project budget; ensuring that team meetings are held and acting as meeting secretary; facilitating team meetings, and coping with much of the project paperwork.

Chose the leader with care. The team leader can be from *any functional department* – there is no evidence that one department versus another produces the best product innovation team leaders. Numerous studies have, however, identified the qualities and characteristics of good project team leaders in product innovation. Sadly, most companies chose the lead person for the wrong reasons, very often for their technical skills or marketing skills. Wrong! Here are the qualities of a good team leader in order of importance, a composite list based on a number of studies:[7]

- Leadership skills
- People skills
- Passion for project (and a vision for project)
- Respected by others; credibility within the organization
- Goal oriented
- Technical skills (such as R&D; or marketing).

Increasingly, progressive companies such as Procter & Gamble, are investing in leadership training. Some (not all) of the desirable characteristics above can be learned, and this team leader training seems to work.

Excellent within-team communication

Effective cross-functional teams feature solid *cooperation* among team members – they really behave like a cohesive team – enabled by superb *within-team communications*, as noted in Exhibit 4.4. In high-productivity businesses, team members are in constant communication with each other. Some practices we observe that help in this communication include:

- *The team leader as chief communicator:* Team leaders must take charge of within-team (as well as outside-the-team) communications. This is an important role of the team leader, and one that poor team leaders often neglect.
- *Weekly meetings of the entire team:* The team leader holds frequent but short meetings at a pre-scheduled time slot. These are timely updates for all team members to review where the team is, what was accomplished last week, what the team needs to do this week, and to appraise team members of issues and agree upon solutions. It helps to keep the team focused.
- *Co-location:* The project team has its own team office. For several days a week, team members relocate to this office from their normal functional locations. This arrangement works, especially in the case of a company where people are physically located within the same city or building.
- *Electronic communication:* Increasingly project teams are global, so they must rely on electronic communication – emails, video and teleconferencing. Some tips and hints: Smart team leaders understand that it is much easier to use emails and teleconferences once people know each other fairly well, so they organize a team-building activity and meeting early in each stage of the project to provide this face-to-face contact

and socialization. A second tip: Video conferencing is not a universal panacea. (It's also expensive, and often the equipment and linkages are problematic.) Indeed many teams report that teleconferencing in combination with Webex or web-networking is more effective than video conferencing. The preferred set-up provides voice communication as well as the needed computer-based visuals. But watching someone's head-and-shoulders on a TV monitor does not add much to the meeting.

- *IT support:* Team performance and communication is improved by the use of a shared information system based on software. Almost four times as many best performing businesses have these information systems in place as poor performing ones, as seen in Exhibit 4.4. For example, Pall Corporation, a global filtration systems manufacturer, reports time savings of 10 percent per team member due to better collaboration and reusing knowledge by employing IT; in this company's case, *Accolade®*.[8] Another user of *Accolade*, J.M. Huber, a chemicals and materials manufacturer, claims that the company eliminates one person-month per year per team member by more efficiently preparing process deliverables and project documentation, the result of using this shared IT information system.[9]

- *Open office designs:* Removal of physical barriers sometimes helps to eliminate communication barriers within an organization. GoJo, a hand-cream company and maker of the big seller *Purelle®*, has removed all interior partitions and walls within their headquarters building in Akron, Ohio, so that all people within the organization co-mingle. Not even the president's desk is enclosed by office walls!

An empowered team

The team and leader must have *authority over their resources* – people and funds – if they are to move their project forward quickly and effectively. Authority or power translates into control over what the team members do with their time (or at least, control of that portion of their time for which they are assigned to the project). In high-productivity businesses,

Exhibit 4.4 More Characteristics of Effective Product Innovation Teams

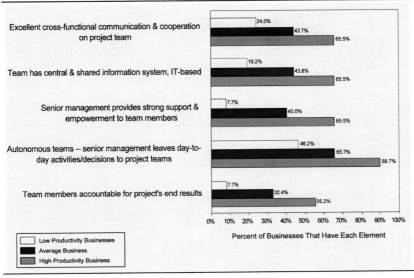

Source: CEK study, endnote 5.

senior management provides strong support for and empowerment of project teams, as shown in Exhibit 4.4. Note the huge difference between best performers and poor performers in terms of this practice. In poor performers, this empowerment and support for the team is missing. Rather, team leaders are most often impotent leaders and leaders in name only; and they are typically second-guessed and have their decisions overruled by functional bosses.

The act of team empowerment occurs at the gates – the Go/Kill decision points in the project. That is, at gates there is a *transfer of power* from functional bosses to the team leader and team. On exiting each gate, not only does the project leader leave the meeting with "approval to move the project forward", he or she also walks out of the gate review with a check in hand – with resources assigned to the project. These resources are people (including person-days and/or a specified percentage of their time) and money. In this way, the project leader acquires the resources required to move his or her project forward, as well as some control over these resources; project team members then report to the team leader by way of a dotted line.

One facet of empowerment is continued *senior management support* for project teams and their leaders. In the best practice businesses, senior people are more than judge and jury. One role is to provide resources to deserving projects and teams. But their role goes further than that: It is also to provide support, encouragement and even *executive sponsorship* to projects, especially the challenging ones. A further role of senior management is to provide *help and mentoring* when needed. Senior management's role is *not* to micro-manage project teams by meddling in the team's effort on a day-to-day basis. Rather – and by a considerable margin in high-productivity businesses – senior management leaves the day-to-day decisions and activities to the project team. They coach team members to think for themselves.

With power and autonomy comes *responsibility*. Thus, in return for resources and partial control over them, the project team and leader are *held accountable* for the project's final results. That is, the results that the team achieves are gauged against promises made at gate reviews by the team and leader. And the full team – all members – is fully responsible for achieving these end results. Note in Exhibit 4.4 that team accountability is a strong best practice that clearly separates the high-productivity businesses from the rest. Seven times as many best performers hold product innovation teams *accountable for the end result* as do poor performers; but a significant minority of the best businesses have some improving to do here! The topic of accountability leads logically into in the next LRP Principle.

Metrics, Accountability and Continuous Improvement: Lean, Rapid and Profitable NPD Principle Number 5

Establishing a culture of *continuous improvement* is one of the main tenets of lean manufacturing, and lends itself readily to application in the field of product innovation. Recall the words of the American philosopher, Santayana: "Those that cannot remember the past are condemned to repeat it." In short, if your business does not make a concerted effort to review past projects, learn from mistakes, and seek ways to improve future projects, you will never get better!

Continuous improvement requires three major components:

1. *Having performance metrics in place.* These metrics answer the questions: How well did you do on that project? and How well are you doing at product innovation generally?

2. *Establishing team accountability for results.* Here the notion is that all members of the project team are fully responsible for performance results when measured against these metrics. Similarly, members of senior management are accountable for achieving product innovation results for the business overall.

3. *Building in learning and improvement.* When the team or business misses the mark, or when deficiencies occur, focus on fixing the cause – stop this from happening again – rather than putting a band-aid on the symptom.

These three components work together to create a learning organization and build in continuous improvement. Metrics are one of the essential components: Without metrics in place, how can you measure whether or not you miss or hit the mark? Metrics and measurement make it possible to spot problems and deficiencies in your product development system or methods, so that corrective action can be taken. Next, metrics take on much more relevance when there is accountability – when someone is charged with achieving the goals against that metric.

Without accountability, metrics lose much of their value and impact. Finally, the continuous learning and improvement facet must be in place too: If results are measured, and deficiencies are identified but no action is taken the system never gets better and you keep repeating the same mistakes.

Many high-productivity businesses embrace this fifth principle of lean, rapid and profitable product innovation as shown in Exhibit 4.5. That is, they put in place performance metrics that measure the success of new products and product development; they hold teams and management accountable for achieving results against these metrics; and they institute improvement efforts when results fall short. Note, however, from Exhibit 4.5 that this is one of the weakest of all principles, with only 28 percent of all businesses embracing metrics, accountability and continuous improvement.[10] Even many high-productivity businesses miss out here, but they still embrace this principle by an almost five-to-one ratio when compared to low-productivity businesses. Clearly this is an area on which most companies can and should seek major improvements – and it is a definite best practice.

Step 1: Put performance metrics in place

You can't manage what you don't measure. Indeed, too many businesses are guilty of not measuring their new product results. For example, it is not clear whether a specific project was a success – whether or not it met its profit or sales targets. And new product results for the entire business are missing: No one knows for sure how well or how badly the business is performing at product innovation.

Top performing businesses put metrics in place, as shown in Exhibit 4.6. And they measure performance in three vital areas:

1. *Individual new product success:* High-productivity businesses, by a three-to-one ratio, measure individual new product performance, when compared to poor performers.
2. *How well the process is working:* Best performers measure how well their product innovation process is working; for example, whether projects

**Exhibit 4.5 Highly Productive Businesses Practice the 5th Principle —
Metrics, Accountability and Continuous Improvement**

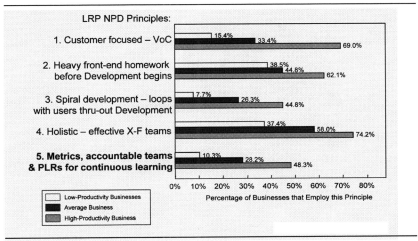

Source: CEK study, endnote 10.

are hitting gates on time; or how well projects are being executed.

3. *Overall business performance in product innovation:* Compared to poor performers, twice as many high-productivity businesses gauge how well their business is performing overall in NPD.

Note from Exhibit 4.6 that the use of metrics is not widespread, especially project and process metrics, with 30 percent or fewer businesses employing such metrics.

The lack of metrics has many ripple effects. For example, without project metrics in place, project teams cannot be held accountable for results. Similarly, senior management cannot be held accountable for their contribution and leadership if there are no metrics that gauge how well the business is performing in product innovation. And without process metrics, there is no consistent identification of weaknesses in the process. All this adds up to a lack of learning and not much in the way of continuous improvement.

Exhibit 4.6 Best Performers Keep Score in Three Areas

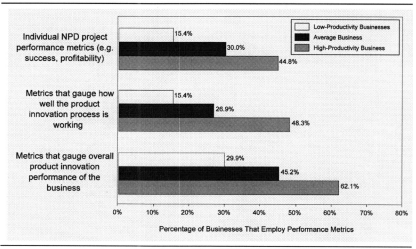

Source: CEK study, endnote 11.

Popular metrics

The most popular metrics to gauge the *performance of individual new product projects* are sales and profit measures, as shown in Exhibit 4.7.[11] Revenue achieved versus forecasted revenue is used the most (70.5 percent of businesses that measure project performance use this metric), followed by profitability (NPV or operating profits). Customer satisfaction is also employed (64.8 percent of businesses) and includes a variety of tools, such as results from satisfaction surveys, warranty claims, returns and complaints tracking. Additionally, a number of businesses rely on project metrics that capture time – either time to market or on-time performance.

When it comes to measuring the *business's overall product innovation performance*, the most popular metric by far is the percentage of revenue derived from new products launched in the last three years.[12] Over two-thirds of businesses employ this metric, as shown in Exhibit 4.8. Other financial metrics, such as percentage of growth from new products and overall profits generated from new products, are also popular.

Exhibit 4.7 Metrics Used to Gauge Individual Project Performance

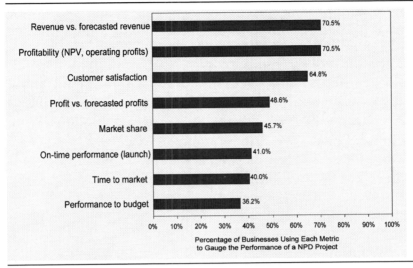

Source: CEK study, endnote 11.

Exhibit 4.8 Metrics Used to Gauge Overall Performance of Business's Total Product Innovation Efforts

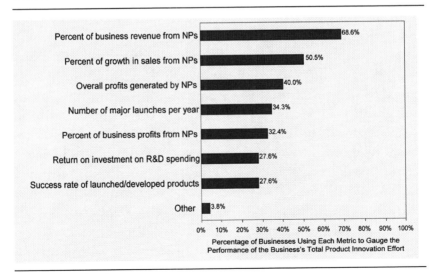

Source: CEK study, endnote 12.

Step 2: Establish success criteria and hold teams accountable

High-productivity businesses measure performance for individual new product projects. They establish *success criteria* for each project and, then, measure how well the project performs against these success criteria. Measurement occurs at gate reviews as well as at the Post Launch Review.

Here is how it works. The project leader and team declare their projections on key performance metrics as part of their business case at Go-to-Development gate. Example projections might be:

- NPV ($000) (or some other profit metric such as EVA)
- Year 1 sales ($000 or units)
- Launch date (or time-to-market).

Additionally the project team may also define some *in-process success criteria*, such as promised product test results or product performance claims. These are important numbers and projections and are a major input into the Go/Kill decision. On the basis of these and other projections, senior management makes the decision to move the project into development, and these projections now become *success criteria*.

The project team is then held accountable for delivering promised results against these success criteria. For example, at successive gates – Go-to-Testing and Go-to-Launch – these same metrics are tracked, and the project team is challenged by gatekeepers: "How is the project faring against these metrics? Is it still in good shape?" And, again, Go/Kill decisions are based in large part on whether or not the project and team continues to meet the stated success criteria. Significant gaps or shortfalls possibly signal a Kill decision at the gate; it could also initiate a problem solving session: Why did this happen? How can this be avoided in the future?

The Post Launch Review is the final *point of accountability* for the project team. Actual results achieved are determined: the first year's sales; the launch date achieved; and the NPV based on latest expected results. These numbers are then compared to the projections – to the *original success criteria*. Accountability issues are high on the agenda of this vital best-practice review: Did the team achieve what was promised when measured against the success criteria?

Benefits of success criteria and accountability

Several key benefits accrue from the use of this success criteria system. First, project teams now have clearly-defined goals – targets that they must achieve. And they can now work towards achieving these targets in a much more purposeful manner – they have a mission! Second, because project teams are held accountable for achieving the numbers, their original projections are much more thoughtful, fact-based and reliable. Gone are the days when project leaders would simply pull a number out of thin air and present it as a "first year sales estimate" – nobody ever tracked the number anyway!

A third benefit is that the emphasis is now shifted from "getting one's project approved" to "winning in the marketplace". Previously, the goal was to present a case to senior management that almost guaranteed that the project would be approved. Thus, overzealous project leaders presented very optimistic numbers to make their projects look more favorable. But leaders were never held accountable for achieving the forecast result, so overly optimistic estimates were the norm. With success criteria and accountability now in place, project leaders must present much more sober and realistic projections, because all eyes are on those estimates until the Post Launch Review – there is accountability.

Another benefit is that the gatekeepers have reasonably reliable projections on which to base their Go/Kill decision. And they can track the project gate to gate against these estimates. So these success criteria become valuable tools for making better Go/Kill decisions. Finally, success or failure after launch can be determined objectively: Did the project hit the numbers originally projected in the success criteria?

Step 3: Practice continuous improvement

High-productivity businesses practice continuous learning and improvement. They learn from their mistakes by seeking feedback from projects and teams at the Post Launch Review, as well as in real time (for example, at gate meetings as projects are progressing).

Some examples:
Toyota holds both real-time and post-mortem learning events (called Hansai or reflection) that encourage functional specialists to validate and update their own knowledge databases.[13]

3M uses Six Sigma approaches to solve new product development problems and prevent their recurrence in projects. The focus here is on improving *quality of execution of activities and tasks* in their NPI new product process.[14]

Post Launch Reviews are vital to providing feedback essential to organization learning. A complete *retrospective analysis* of the project takes place, where the project team reviews their steps and actions in their just-completed project. The question is: What can we learn here? This exercise provides the essential organizational learning.

Best practice suggests that you install *two reviews* after launch as shown in Exhibit 4.9. The first is an interim review that occurs a month or two after launch, designed to provide a first look at early commercial results, and to decide on course corrections and fixes needed in the early days of launch.

Conducting a retrospective analysis

This first post launch review is also an ideal point to conduct the post-mortem or *retrospective analysis* of the project. Here the project team gathers in a room with all their project notes, lab books and project e-mails while the project is still fresh in their minds. Using a long roll of

Real Life Examples of Improvements Made as a Result of Continuous Improvements and Post Launch Reviews

1. Eliminating expensive work undertaken too early. Example:
   - Physical prototypes were being developed far too early in the process in order to provide something to show the customer.
   Improvement made: Now, virtual prototypes are developed by CAD which is more effective, cheaper and faster for concept testing.
2. Eliminating the need to seek approvals from many committees. Examples:
   - *Problem:* The project leader was previously required to make presentations to Environmental, Safety, Legal and Color Committees before appearing at some gate meetings.
   Improvement made: Now, committees either sign off on the project beforehand, or the committee's ultimate boss attends the gate meeting.
   - *Problem:* As the project moved into the commercialization stage, the project team was required to seek project approval first at a gate meeting, and then seek a second approval at a CAPEX committee meeting for capital equipment.
   Improvement made: By integrating the CAPEX process into the new product process, this time-consuming two-step decision situation was eliminated. Several CAPEX committee reps now attend the gate meeting.
3. Synchronizing the new product process with other company processes and decision systems. Examples:
   - Design engineering was synchronized with manufacturing engineering so that hand-off problems were minimized.
   - When first introduced, Six Sigma clashed with the already well-established new product process. Now Six Sigma and DFSS have become a tool to use *within* the new product process.
   - The Decision-to-Launch gate was linked to the standard operating procedure for the plant; namely, "release to manufacture". Previously, there had been disconnects.

paper – perhaps 20 feet or seven meters long – they sketch out a blow by blow historical walk-through of their recently completed project from idea to launch. They then go back over the entire map, lower the microscope on each stage and activity, and pose four key questions:

- What was done in this step or activity?
- How proficient was the execution?
- How can this step or activity be improved – how could we have done it better?
- How could we do it faster (in the event of lengthy activities)?

The goal is that every project will be done better than the one before! By conducting such retrospective analyses after the launch of every new product, problems in the project are pinpointed; systemic errors and deficiencies are identified (recurring errors and problems with projects generally); and possible solutions are suggested. When gaps, problems and weaknesses are identified, problem-solving sessions are held which focus on root causes. The approach is to fix the cause, not the symptom! And corrective actions designed to stop future recurrence are identified. Learning and continuous improvement become an integral and routine facet of the development process.

The Final Post Launch Review

The final Post Launch Review takes place approximately one year after launch and when some commercial results are known. It is the final review of the project with the gatekeepers, the same senior managers who approved the project in the first place (and the group with whom the project leader established the original success criteria). It closes the loop! Here, team and project performance is gauged against the original success criteria. And when gaps and problems are identified, corrective actions are taken to fix the systematic problems and deficiencies in the process that led to these gaps.

Exhibit 4.9 Build in Post Launch Reviews

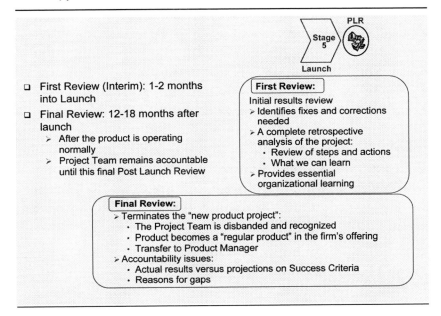

- First Review (Interim): 1-2 months into Launch
- Final Review: 12-18 months after launch
  - After the product is operating normally
  - Project Team remains accountable until this final Post Launch Review

First Review:
Initial results review
- Identifies fixes and corrections needed
- A complete retrospective analysis of the project:
  - Review of steps and actions
  - What we can learn
- Provides essential organizational learning

Final Review:
- Terminates the "new product project":
  - The Project Team is disbanded and recognized
  - Product becomes a "regular product" in the firm's offering
  - Transfer to Product Manager
- Accountability issues:
  - Actual results versus projections on Success Criteria
  - Reasons for gaps

This Post Launch Review also terminates the new product project; success or failure is determined, and the project leader and team are recognized for their efforts. Note that the project team *remains accountable* for the project *until this final Post Launch Review* takes place.

Building in the lessons

Who oversees these Post Launch Reviews? The majority of high-productivity businesses already have a *Stage-Gate® Process Manager in place to champion and guide the idea-to-launch process.*[15] One of their key roles is to ensure that learning and continuous improvement occurs. They do this by overseeing the Post Launch Reviews, and by staying on top of problems as projects progress. The Stage-Gate Process Manager facilitates these sessions, captures the problems and lessons learned, works to prevent their recurrence, and incorporates the lessons into the organization.

The Stage-Gate Process Manager must take action. With benefit of the lessons learned at these post launch reviews, he or she:

- modifies the product innovation process by incorporating the new insights and learnings
- builds the lessons into the company's training sessions
- includes the lessons in the business's *inventory of best practices*, and
- coaches the other project teams on these new insights and lessons.

Where a systemic problem is identified (one that occurs across a number of projects), which a single project team or the Process Manager cannot solve alone, often the Process Manager establishes a "working group" or a "community of excellence" to tackle and solve the problem, thus preventing its recurrence.

Install a Post Launch Review

The model makes sense: establish metrics; hold teams accountable for achieving these results on these metrics; and when gaps, deficiencies and problems occur, take action to prevent their recurrence. The problem is that most businesses do not even hold a Post Launch Review. They never go back and determine whether the team achieved their promised results, or review what happened in the project, and identify what improvements are needed. Exhibit 4.10 shows the worst executed activities of the entire new product process.[16] Not surprisingly, market research in the early stages is the weakest activity, followed by idea generation. But the Post Launch Review is a close third: Only 22 percent of businesses conduct a proficient Post Launch Review. But note that by a six-to-one ratio, high-productivity businesses undertake this Post Launch Review well; and they get the benefit of continuous improvement as well as team accountability. This is a clear best practice, but it is also an area where most businesses are very weak.

Exhibit 4.10 The Worst Executed Activities in Product Innovation Projects

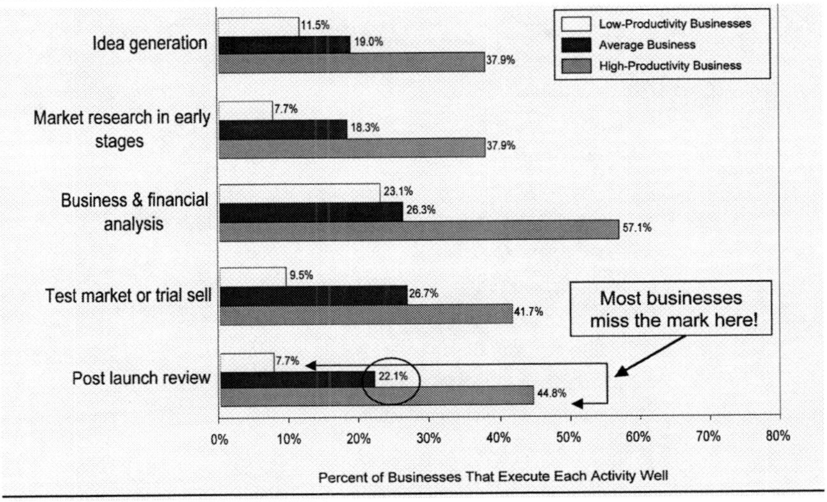

Percent of Businesses That Execute Each Activity Well

Source: CEK study, endnote 16.

Conclusion

You have seen two more principles of *Lean, Rapid and Profitable New Product Development* – they are summarized in Exhibit 4.11 as Principles Numbers 4 and 5. Both principles deal with effectively driving the new product project to market. The principle of a holistic process driven by a true cross-functional team is fundamental to success in product innovation. But many companies have not embraced this principle well – there is much room for improvement. The principle of metrics, accountable teams, and continuous improvement – borrowed largely from the field of lean manufacturing – is essential if promised results are to be achieved, and if your new product system is to be an *evergreen process*, constantly renewing and improving to yield even better results. Implement these two principles – they strongly distinguish the high-productivity business from the rest.

Now read on and learn about the sixth principle, and one so profound and high-impact that we devote an entire chapter to the topic: Making the right investment decisions for effective portfolio management.

Exhibit 4.11 Summary — The Seven Principles of LRP NPD

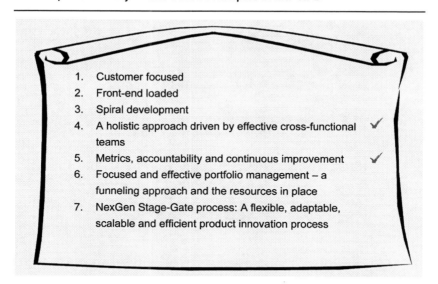

1. Customer focused
2. Front-end loaded
3. Spiral development
4. A holistic approach driven by effective cross-functional teams ✓
5. Metrics, accountability and continuous improvement ✓
6. Focused and effective portfolio management – a funneling approach and the resources in place
7. NexGen Stage-Gate process: A flexible, adaptable, scalable and efficient product innovation process

Maximizing Productivity in Your Portfolio

Lean Rapid and Profitable NPD Principle Number 6

Focus and Effective Portfolio Management[1]

There are two ways to improve productivity in NPD. The first is by emphasizing *doing projects right*, for example executing projects better and faster. That is what Principles number 1 to number 5 in the last few chapters have been about. If you are indeed customer focused, front-end load your projects, practice fast-paced spiral development, adopt a holistic cross-functional approach, and build in metrics, accountability and continuous improvement, your business surely will improve the productivity of its product innovation projects!

The other way to improve productivity is to *do the right projects* – to revise your investment portfolio by choosing better and different innovation projects to invest in. That is, change the character, balance and mix of your portfolio away from low value, low productivity areas and projects and towards high productivity, high value areas and projects. That is what portfolio management is all about.[2] It's a term that we borrow from the investment community, where the profession of *portfolio manager* has been around for many years, but it has only recently been introduced to the field of product innovation.

High-productivity businesses practice effective portfolio management much more so than do poor performers – by more than a four-to-one ratio, as shown in Exhibit 5.1.[3] That is, they install *a systematic portfolio management system* which ensures the right balance and mix of projects in the portfolio and helps to select the right projects to invest in. A closer look at Exhibit 5.1 reveals that effective portfolio management is an elusive goal for many firms, however, and is the *weakest of the six principles* outlined so far. So there is much room for productivity improvements here. A significant number of businesses – the 40 percent high-productivity businesses that do practice effective portfolio management – show us this can be achieved, and they provide insights into effective portfolio management methods.

What is portfolio management?

Recognize that every product innovation project is an investment. Like stock market investments, these development investments must be carefully scrutinized and focused through an *effective portfolio management system*. Portfolio management is about effective resource allocation and addresses the question: How should your business invest its R&D or development funds and people? In short, what should be your NPD or development investment portfolio?

One facet of portfolio management deals with issues of balance in the portfolio – resource allocation across markets, technologies, product-types and project-types. A second facet of portfolio management is making decisions about which new products and other development projects your business should fund from among many opportunities – Go/Kill decisions.

Exhibit 5.1 Focused and Effective Portfolio Management — Highly Productive Businesses Practice the 6th Principle

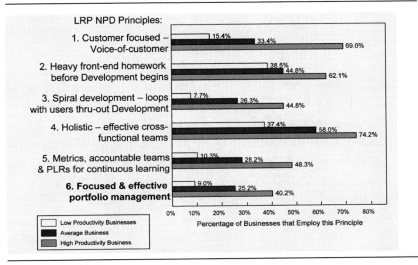

Source: CEK study, endnote 3.

A Dramatic Downward Trend in Recent Portfolios

From 1995 to 2004, product development cycle times in the United States have decreased from 41.7 months to 24 months.[4] This represents an astounding 42 percent decrease in time-to-market in ten years! How? What's going on here? Have you really become that much more efficient at product innovation? Or is some other factor at play here?[5]

Another dramatic trend is that while time-to-market is down, NPD productivity is also down! New product sales fell from 32.6 percent of total company sales in the mid 1990s to 28 percent in 2004, according to a major PDMA study.[6] The same study shows that profits derived from new products are down from 33.2 percent of business profits to 28.3 percent over the same period.

Why are results down?

These significant decreases in sales and profits from new products in just a handful of years are cause for concern. New products remain a major component in corporate revenue and profits. But something is happening to make them a smaller portion of that revenue and profit.

There is no evidence that people are doing a worse job today – poor market studies, bad launches, or deficient design and development work. Indeed, a comparison of the quality of execution of key activities between 1985 and today – from initial screening through to market launch – reveals no change in quality ratings.[7] And R&D spending in the United States remains pretty much unchanged; for example, 2.76 percent of GNP in 1985 versus 2.82 percent in 2001.

The one factor that does show a dramatic change, however, and that explains the decrease in productivity as well as the huge reduction in time-to-market, is *the mix in the portfolio of projects undertaken today versus in 1990.* Simply stated, today businesses are preoccupied with minor modifications, product tweaks, and minor responses to salespeople's requests, while *true product development has taken a back seat.* Look at the facts shown in Exhibit 5.2.

Companies undertook almost twice as many "new to world" or true innovation projects in 1990 as they do today as a percentage of their development portfolios, according to our benchmarking data.[8] Now things are reversed. Today, businesses undertake almost twice as many minor projects – improvements, modifications and tweaks – as they did in 1990.

These trends are also evident in the PDMA study, which reveals that "the number of projects motivated by cost reduction, repositionings and incremental improvements has grown, while the percentage of major revisions, product-line additions, new to the firm and new-to-the-world projects has dropped."[9] For example, new-to-world and new-to-firm projects have decreased from 30 percent of the portfolio in 1995 to 25 percent in nine short years – a 17 percent decrease. This explains why cycle times have decreased so dramatically, from 41.7 months to

Exhibit 5.2 Breakdown of the Portfolio by Project Types — Then and Now

Development Project Type	% of Projects in the Development Portfolio		
	1990	2004	% Change from 1990
New to world, new to market – innovations	20.4%	11.5%	43.7% decrease
New product lines to the company	38.8	27.1	30.1% decrease
Additions to existing product line in company	20.4	24.7	20.8% increase
Improvements & modifications to existing company products	20.4	36.7	80.1% increase
Total	100.0%	100.0%	

Source: *Visions*, endnote 5; and CEK study, endnote 3.

24 months. Businesses are not undertaking the challenging, step-out and significant innovations and new products they once did. They are focusing on incremental improvements which inherently take less time – a trivialization of NPD.

Major problems with portfolios

Astute executives in some businesses recognize the dangers, and are concerned about their low-productivity portfolios, as shown in Exhibit 5.3. Managements in only 21.2 percent of businesses indicate that their development portfolios contain enough *high value-to-the-corporation projects*. And only 19.4 percent of business managements claim that their portfolio has the *right balance* between short term and long term projects[10]. And there is more: There are *far too many projects* for the limited resources available in the great majority of firms, and most businesses confess to doing a *poor job of ranking and prioritizing* product innovation projects. Finally, only a small minority of businesses have a *systematic and formal portfolio management process* in place.

Exhibit 5.3 Some More Provocative Portfolio Facts

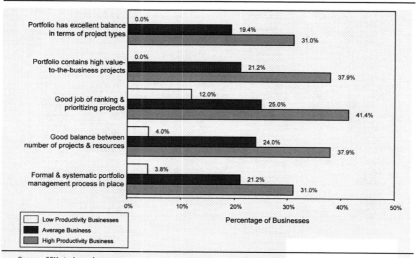

Source: CEK study, endnote 10.

All of these deficiencies drive productivity down! Note from Exhibit 5.3, however, that high-productivity businesses suffer much less from these deficiencies. The top performing businesses fare much better on these portfolio metrics, often by ratios of more than ten-to-one when compared to poor performers.

Portfolio Management: Fundamental to Improving Productivity

Effective portfolio management in product innovation, just as in the stock market, is fundamental to maximizing productivity or yields. Recall that productivity is defined as maximum bang for buck, or more formally as:

$$\text{Productivity} = \frac{\text{Output}}{\text{Input}}$$

When measured across your entire development portfolio, this translates into what your development projects yield in terms of sales and profits when compared to how much you spend in terms of money and people to achieve this.

Increasing Productivity in the Portfolio

There are three basic ways to employ portfolio management to improve the productivity of your product innovation investments:

1. *Strategic.* The first route to improve productivity is via *strategic portfolio management.* The approach here is to focus your resources away from low-productivity areas and to areas which offer greater promise. This is analogous to the farmer spreading seed preferentially on fertile fields. The unwise farmer spreads seed indiscriminately over both unfertile and fertile fields, and the yields are often disappointing. Like the unwise farmer, too many businesses spend their precious development resources in many areas – markets, product areas and project types – where the yield is low. In short, the productivity or yield – output over input – of these areas all but guarantees that the portfolio will have a low productivity.

   The farmer has an advantage over the business manager, however, because the farmer *measures his yields* per acre from different fields. By contrast, the product innovation manager tends to have very poor metrics in place to measure product development results, such as yield or productivity, as we saw in the last chapter!

   To summarize, the strategic portfolio approach is to *shift the balance of projects* in terms of key strategic dimensions to areas that offer a greater yield or productivity. These strategic dimensions include, for example: markets or business sectors, product lines or categories, technology types, and project types.

2. *Tactical.* The second route to improve productivity is more tactical, namely astute *project prioritization and selection.* Once you have decided on the right areas, mix and balance, now the task is to judiciously pick the best projects within each area. This requires a

systematic method for *evaluating, ranking and prioritizing your projects* or investment opportunities. You prioritize the list of active and on-hold projects, with the highest productivity projects at the top of the list. By selecting the top half or top two-thirds of the list, you thus maximize the productivity of the portfolio. The challenge is, of course, to figure out how to effectively prioritize a list of projects, when often the information available on each is fairly limited and quite uncertain. Hint: Professional portfolio managers in the financial community rely on well-crafted systems for evaluating and making their stock and bond selections. When it comes to product innovation investments, maybe these folks can teach us a thing or two. Most businesses are a long way from having anything that resembles a systematic project evaluation and prioritization method.

3. *Putting a limit on the number of projects.* As seen in Exhibit 5.3, most businesses have far too many projects in their portfolios for the resources available. This does serious damage to productivity by creating huge delays (projects waiting in a queue for someone to get around to working on them; or worse yet, pipeline gridlock, with nothing moving very fast at all). Long times-to-market hurt productivity, as revenues are deferred. Another negative consequence is that, with too many projects underway, project teams cut corners and often execute poorly as a result; and so the new product underperforms, and productivity suffers again.

   Putting a limit on the number of projects avoids pipeline gridlock, and enables the remaining or selected projects to be properly resourced and thus to be accelerated to market. Time to market is reduced, revenues are realized earlier, the project is executed better, and the productivity is increased. While many firms do attempt to balance resources with numbers of projects, the sad fact is that most businesses lack the discipline to say "no". The message is that you must learn to *drown some puppies* and prune some of the less critical or less valuable projects out of your portfolio.

A hierarchical decision process[11]

Portfolio management and resource allocation can thus be treated as a hierarchical process, with two levels of decision-making (see Exhibit 5.4):[12]

> *Level 1 – Strategic portfolio management:* Strategic portfolio decisions answer the question: Directionally, where should your business spend its innovation resources (people and funds)? How should you split your resources across projects types, markets, technologies or product categories? And on what major initiatives or new platforms should you concentrate your resources? Establishing *strategic buckets* and defining *strategic product roadmaps* are effective tools here (more on these methods follow).

> *Level 2 – Tactical portfolio decisions* (project prioritization and project selection): Tactical portfolio decisions focus on individual projects, but obviously follow from the strategic decisions. They address the question: Which specific projects should you do? Such decisions are shown at the bottom part of Exhibit 5.4, while tools for these tactical decisions are outlined later in this chapter.

Strategic Buckets

Many best performing companies use the concept of *strategic buckets* to help in the resource deployment decisions. Strategic buckets simply define where management desires the innovation dollars to go, broken down by project type, by market, by geography, and/or by product area.[13] Strategic buckets are based on the notion that *strategy becomes real when you start spending money*, and thus translating strategy from theory to reality is about making decisions on where the resources should be spent; thus, strategic buckets. In use, management begins with the business' strategy and then makes strategic choices about resource allocation (as shown in Exhibit 5.5): How many resources go to new products versus improvements, modifications and extensions versus platform developments?

Exhibit 5.4 Strategic and Tactical Portfolio Management — Both Are Used to Increase Portfolio Productivity

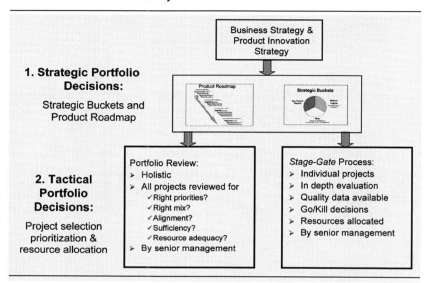

Then projects are categorized by bucket, and subsequently rank-ordered within each bucket.

The illustration in Exhibit 5.6 shows strategic buckets in use. Here, management has made strategic choices about resource allocation, deciding on the proportion of resources going to each project type or bucket – "new products" versus "improvements and modifications" versus "cost reductions" versus "marketing/salesforce requests". (For illustration in Exhibit 5.6, these resource allocations are rounded to $2M, $3M, $2M and $3M respectively).

With resource allocation now firmly established and driven by strategy, projects within each bucket are then ranked against each other, until one is out of resources in each bucket, as shown in the four lists in Exhibit 5.6. This establishes project priorities within each bucket.

Note that projects in one bucket – such as "new products" – do not compete against projects in another bucket, such as "improvements and modifications." If they did, in the short term, simple and inexpensive projects would always win out, as they do in many businesses (most

Exhibit 5.5 Use Strategic Buckets to Obtain the Right Balance of Projects

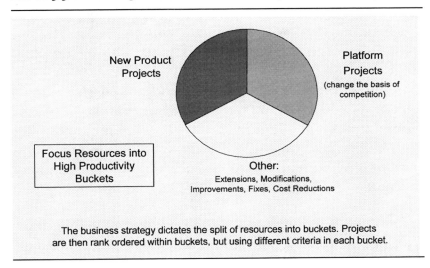

The business strategy dictates the split of resources into buckets. Projects are then rank ordered within buckets, but using different criteria in each bucket.

Exhibit 5.6 Using Strategic Buckets

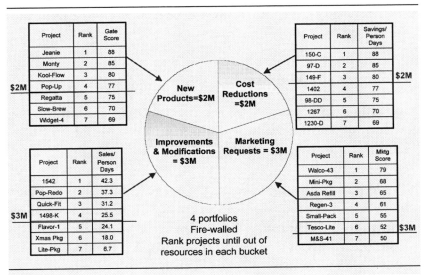

companies have far too many of the smaller "low hanging fruit" projects and not nearly enough of bolder and genuine new product projects).[14] Instead, strategic buckets *build firewalls between buckets.* By earmarking specific amounts to "new products" and to "platform developments," the portfolio becomes much more balanced.

In spite of its intuitive appeal, the use of strategic buckets is a decidedly weak area overall with only 27 percent of businesses developing strategic buckets, as shown in Exhibit 5.7. But strategic buckets is clearly a best practice, with almost three times as many best performers (41 percent) employing this strategic buckets approach when compared to worst performers.

Strategic buckets apply not only to project types, as in both Exhibit 5.5 and 5.6. There are other dimensions that are strategic, and splits or buckets can be created using these as well. For example, the illustration in Exhibit 5.8 shows a business that splits resources by product line and by market segment, addressing the two key questions:

- What proportion of R&D resources should go to each of the four product lines?
- What should be the split in R&D resources across the five major market segments the business operates in?

Deciding the size of strategic buckets

Many factors must be considered by senior management when deciding how many resources each strategic bucket receives. As Exhibit 5.9 illustrates, these factors or inputs include:

1. *Strategy and goals:* The business strategy, and from that its product innovation and technology goals and strategy, have a huge bearing on where the money or resources should be spent. The *size of the buckets must reflect the strategic priorities of the business.* The problem here is that a minority of companies have actually crafted a product innovation and technology strategy. For example, from Exhibit 5.7, note that only 38.1 percent of businesses have clearly articulated goals for their

Exhibit 5.7 Best Performing Businesses Develop a Product Innovation & Technology Strategy

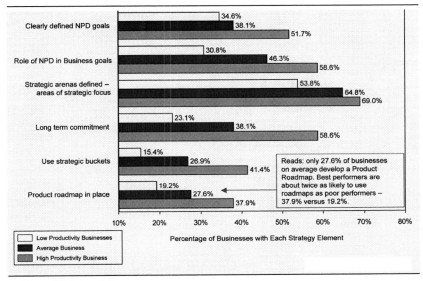

Source: CEK study, endnote 3.

Exhibit 5.8 Use Other Dimensions to Split Resources

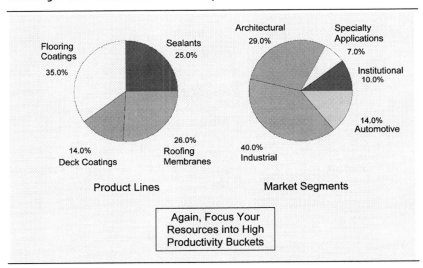

total product innovation effort. A higher proportion (64.8 percent) have defined strategic arenas – areas of focus for their product innovation efforts. Thus, mapping out a product innovation and technology strategy for your business may be the first order of business!

2. *Benchmark data:* Best-in-class businesses also provide an indication of where the money should be spent. Some companies benchmark best performers in their respective industries to acquire guides as to spending splits. The portfolio breakdown of high-productivity businesses across a broad array of industries is:[15]
   - New to world, new to your market (true innovations)   17%
   - New product lines to the company   26%
   - New items in existing company product lines   27%
   - Improvements and modifications of existing
     company products   30%

   Note that this is a breakdown by project numbers and not resource splits. Strategic buckets should deal with resource splits.

3. *Where the resources were spent in previous years:* One never begins with a clean slate – there is always spending history to consider. Previous spending splits must be considered. For one thing, these historic splits indicate where your talents lie. It is usually not possible to make sweeping changes in the portfolio breakdown, simply because you cannot transfer people and skills seamlessly from one type of project, product type or market to another. But you can make significant directional changes.

4. *The yield from previous years' efforts:* Measure your yields from investments in different areas from previous years. Like the farmer measuring yields from different fields, so you should consider previous yields as a key input for where you invest in the future.

An example of yield or productivity analysis is given in Exhibits 5.10 and 5.11. In the first exhibit, the portfolio manager measures where the funds were spent in previous years in terms of project types (bottom right

Exhibit 5.9 Inputs to the Strategic Buckets Decision

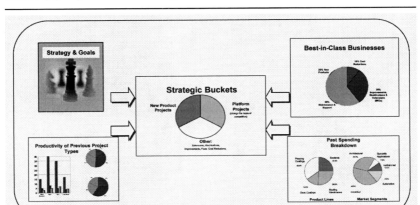

pie chart in Exhibit 5.10). Note that new products received a minority of funds, about 23 percent of the total. Now output is measured: what those same investments yield. Here, three years' cumulative sales were used as the output metric. These outputs are shown in the top right pie chart. Note that new products are somewhat more productive, creating 33 percent of the sales.* Finally the Productivity Index or PI is computed – output or sales divided by input or spending. And the results, shown in the vertical bar chart, are revealing, with new products having the highest yield or productivity (about 7:1) and marketing and sales requests having the least (at 3:1). Such data proves invaluable in deciding next year's spending splits.

A similar chart from the same company shows spending broken down by business area (product lines) in Exhibit 5.11. This chart reveals even more provocative results, with the traditional product line of the business – which we disguised and labeled as Business Area C – receiving more

---

* Savings from cost reductions are converted into "equivalent three year sales" by considering three years of savings, and applying a typical profit margin.

Exhibit 5.10 Determine Your Productivity By Project Types

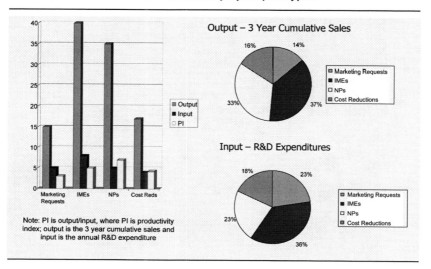

Exhibit 5.11 Productivity By Business Areas

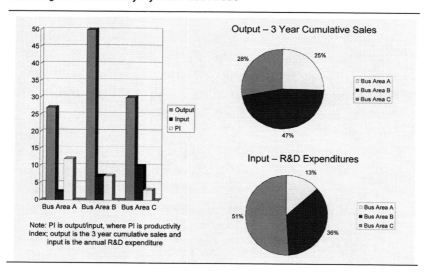

than half the R&D budget, but generating only 28 percent of the sales revenue from development projects. Its Productivity Index is one-quarter of that of Business Area A, which receives little funding. This does not mean that one shifts all the spending to Business Area A, and cuts Business Area C off completely, but it does signal that some shift in resources is needed.

Strategic Buckets: Recap

Using the strategic buckets approach to allocate resources requires that your company have a business strategy and, within that, a product innovation and technology strategy. Such a strategy should specify product innovation goals for your business, define arenas of strategic focus (where you'll focus your R&D or NPD efforts as a business), and the relative priorities of these arenas, as noted in Exhibit 5.7.

Next, strategic buckets require a defined management process that moves from your strategy through to spending decisions or splits by bucket, as noted in Exhibit 5.9. Dimensions (splits) can be anything that is relevant to senior management, with most businesses using four or fewer dimensions concurrently. These dimensions include:

- Project types (as in Exhibits 5.5 and 5.6)
- Product line, product category or product type (as in Exhibit 5.8, left pie chart)
- Market, market segments, business areas or industry sectors (as in Exhibit 5.8, right pie chart)
- Geography (regions of the world)
- Technology or technology type (such as base, pacing or embryonic).

Note: The strategic buckets approach is not merely producing pie charts that show where the resources were expended over the last years, as in Exhibits 5.10 or 5.11. Rather, strategic buckets is very much *future-oriented*, and deals with the issue of *where the resources should go* for the year ahead to help ensure your organization will achieve its growth objectives.

The Strategic Product Roadmap[16]

A strategic roadmap is an effective way to map out a series of major development initiatives in an attack plan; hence, it provides a tentative but longer term view of future resource commitments. A roadmap is simply a management group's view of how to get where they want to go or to achieve their desired objective.[17] Although gaining in popularity, especially in high-technology businesses, the use of roadmaps is a weak area generally, with only 27 percent of businesses developing product roadmaps (shown in Exhibit 5.7). About twice as many best performers (38 percent) use product roadmaps versus worst performers (19 percent).

In use, your business' senior management maps out the planned assaults – the *major product innovation initiatives* and their timing – that are required in order to succeed in a certain market or sector in the form of a *strategic product roadmap.* *This roadmap may also specify the platform developments required for these new initiatives. An illustration of a roadmap (based on a process equipment manufacturer) is shown in Exhibit 5.12, where major development initiatives are laid out over time (often as far out as 5-8 years). Placemarks are established for these development initiatives, and resources are tentatively earmarked for them. In this way, senior management is able to translate its view of the future and its strategy into resource commitments and concrete actions. Additionally, the development or acquisition of new technologies can be mapped out in the form of a *technology roadmap.*†

---

* The term "product roadmap" has come to have many meanings in business. Here we mean a *strategic* roadmap, which lays out the major initiatives and platform developments that the business will undertake well into the future, as opposed to a tactical roadmap, which lists each and every product, extension, modification, tweak, etc.

† The term "technology roadmap" also has several different meanings. Here we use the term to denote your business's technological developments or technology acquisitions; by contrast, the term "technology roadmap" is sometimes used to describe what new technologies are anticipated in an industry – more of an industry technological forecast.

Exhibit 5.12 The Strategic Product Roadmap Lays Out the Major Development Initiatives

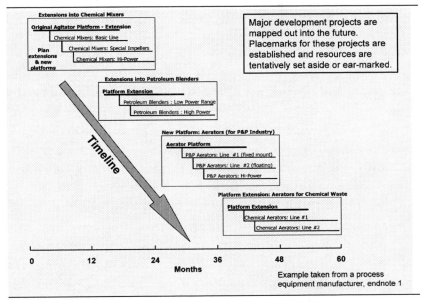

Tactical Portfolio Management – Project Selection[18]

Once these strategic portfolio decisions are made, management can then deal with the next level of decision making: translating strategy into reality.[19] The goal again is to maximize the productivity of the portfolio. The route is by doing fewer but better projects (higher value), and in so doing, driving these selected projects to market as quickly as possible, then moving on to the next ones. Prioritization and making Go/Kill decisions are at the heart of effective tactical portfolio management.

Tactical portfolio decisions focus on projects and address the questions: Which specific new product and development projects should you do? What are their relative priorities? And what resources should be allocated to each? Such tactical decisions are shown at the bottom part of Exhibit 5.4.

To make effective tactical decisions, best performers use a combination of *gates* and *portfolio reviews*, both working in harmony as shown in Exhibit 5.4. Let's look at each one.

Gates: Embedded within your idea-to-launch innovation system should be tough Go/Kill decision-points called *gates*. Gates provide an *in-depth review of individual projects* one at a time, and render Go/Kill, prioritization and resource allocation decisions. Hence, gates must be part of your portfolio management system (bottom right of Exhibit 5.4).

Selecting higher productivity projects at gates is achieved through a focused or funneling approach, as illustrated in Exhibit 5.13: You begin with many solid innovation concepts and successively remove the weak or lower productivity projects via a series of screenings or pruning decisions at the gates. The end result is fewer projects, but higher value projects to the company, and a significant increase in product innovation productivity.

Portfolio Reviews: Doing the *right projects* is more than simply individual project selection at gate meetings; rather, it is about the *entire mix* of projects and innovation or technology investments that your business makes. Therefore, many businesses install a second decision process; namely, the periodic *portfolio review* (bottom left of Exhibit 5.4). Senior management meets two-to-four times per year to review the portfolio of all projects. Here, senior management also makes prioritization decisions, where *all projects* are considered on the table together. Key issues and questions are:

- Are all projects strategically aligned (fit your business's strategy)?
- Do you have the right priorities among projects?
- Are there some projects on the active list that you should kill? Or perhaps accelerate?
- Is there the right balance of projects? The right mix?
- Are there enough resources to do all these projects?
- Do you have sufficiency – if you do these projects, will you achieve your stated business goals?
- What projects, if any, should be placed on hold pending resource availability?

Exhibit 5.13 The Development Funnel Leading to a Tunnel

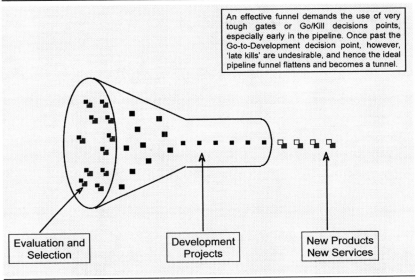

An effective funnel demands the use of very tough gates or Go/Kill decisions points, especially early in the pipeline. Once past the Go-to-Development decision point, however, 'late kills' are undesirable, and hence the ideal pipeline funnel flattens and becomes a tunnel.

Evaluation and Selection

Development Projects

New Products New Services

Project Selection and Prioritization Tools

A myriad of tools exists to select and prioritize development projects, and often the choice of method depends on the type of project. Note: when using strategic buckets, as in Exhibit 5.6, multiple portfolios are the result, one for each project type; and each portfolio or list can *utilize its own prioritization method*. Project selection and prioritization tools are outlined next.

Financial or NPV

NPV, EVA or payback period are traditional and popular metrics and methods to make Go/Kill decisions at gates, and even to rank projects from best to worst. An illustration is provided in Exhibit 5.14.* At your gate meetings, all six projects in Exhibit 5.14 pass your financial hurdles: positive NPV and the IRR (not shown) greater than your company hurdle.

Assuming that all projects must be done in one year, and with an annual development budget of $15 million, it is clear that you cannot do all six projects, Alpha to Foxtrot. So rank your projects according to their value to the company, in this case the NPV. Foxtrot followed by Beta are your top two projects and coincidentally consume all your $15 million of resources. Thus, your portfolio decision is: Undertake two projects – Foxtrot and Beta. These two projects take the entire budget of $15 million, and yield a portfolio value of $115 million. This yields an over-all portfolio Productivity Index of 7.67, which is quite good!

A useful modification of the NPV approach is to adjust for risk. One risk adjustment is to simply apply a probability estimate to each uncertain variable – for example to expected sales – to either inflate or deflate the number. A more legitimate method is to use discount rates that are probability-adjusted (different discount rates for different classes of projects depending on risk level). Your finance department should be able to supply the suggested discount rates for different project types.

Productivity index

A valuable twist on the traditional NPV and a modification designed to *maximize the productivity* of your portfolio is the use of the *Productivity Index*.[20] Here, take what you are trying to maximize (for example, the NPV) and divide by the constraining resource (for example the person-days or development dollars needed to complete the project), as defined in Exhibit 5.15. In practice, the portfolio manager simply calculates the Productivity Index for each project (for example, NPV/person-days per

---

* NPV is the *net present value*, the economic value of the project to the business in $000. The EVA is the *economic value added*, another version of the profitability calculation, and similar to the NPV. The *payback period* indicates the number of years to recover your initial investment. All are standard outputs of a financial spreadsheet; your finance department should develop such a template for your projects.

Exhibit 5.14 Ranking Product Innovation Projects Using NPV

Six Projects: A Major Materials Company						
Project	PV (present value of future earnings)	Development Cost	Commercialization Cost	NPV (net present value)	Ranking Based on NPV	Decision
Alpha	36	3	5	28	4	Hold
Beta	64	5	2	57	2	Go
Gamma	11	2	1	8	5	Hold
Delta	3	1	0.5	1.5	6	Hold
Echo	56	5	3	48	3	Hold
Foxtrot	66	10	2	58	1	Go

Note: Total Development Budget of $15 M

project) and ranks your projects using this index until you run out of resources. This method yields a higher overall value of your portfolio – NPV is maximized for a given resource expenditure – and at the same time, ensures that you do not have too many projects in your development pipeline for the limited resources available.

Consider the illustration in Exhibit 5.16, which displays the same list of six projects. This time you rank them according to their Productivity Index (PI= NPV/Development Cost). Using this Productivity Index, the portfolio decision is different, as more efficient projects are selected: Beta, Echo and Alpha. Note that Foxtrot, previously your number one project, drops entirely off the list! You have used up $13 million of the $15 million budget, so top up the list with project Gamma at a cost of $2 million, for a total spend of $15 million.

The new portfolio value is now $141 million, an increase of $26 million versus the straight NPV method in Exhibit 5.14, with no increase in spending! The Portfolio Productivity Index is now 9.40, up from 7.67 – a significant improvement gained from the astute use of the Productivity Index.

Exhibit 5.15 The Productivity Index Defined

- ❑ Take what you are trying to maximize
  - ➤ Example: NPV
- ❑ Divide by what the constraining resource is
  - ➤ Example: People (expressed as person-days)
  - ➤ Or Development funds ($000)
- ❑ And rank your projects by this index until out of resources

$$\frac{\text{Productivity}}{\text{Index}} = \frac{\text{Output}}{\text{Input}} = \frac{\text{NPV}}{\text{Person-Days}}$$

NPV= forecasted NPV of the project

$$\text{Or} = \frac{\text{NPV}}{\text{Development Cost}}$$

Person-Days = resources required to complete the project

Development Cost = cost to complete the project (the "go forward" costs)

Exhibit 5.16 Use the Productivity Index to Rank Your Projects

Note: Same Total Development Budget of $15 M

Project	NPV	Development Cost	Productivity Index=NPV/ Development Cost	Sum of Development Costs
Beta	57	5	11.4	5
Echo	48	5	9.6	10
Alpha	28	3	9.3	13 **Limit reached**
Foxtrot	58	10	5.8	23
Gamma	8	2	4.0	25
Delta	1.5	1	1.5	26

Real options

Real options (sometime called options pricing theory or expected commercial value) is a variant of the financial models and is designed to *appropriately handle risk and uncertainty.* Of course, every product innovation project has some risk. There is never a 100 percent chance of either technical success or commercial success. Thus, the pundits argue that any method that fails to accommodate the inherent risk in a financial analysis is naïve. One approach to real options is to use decision-tree analysis – breaking the project into a series of steps or stages, each step with several outcomes, success or failure, as displayed in Exhibit 5.17. The consequences of each outcome or tree-branch are determined, and probabilities of each outcome occurring are estimated.

We use data from project Alpha from Exhibit 5.14 as the illustration in Exhibit 5.17. But this time we estimate that the probability of commercial success on launch is only 50 percent, and the probability of technical success in development is 80 percent. Now follow the decision-tree in Exhibit 5.17, beginning with a value of $36 million if successful (far right side), all the way back to the beginning of the project on the left, where the expected commercial value (ECV) is now computed to be only $7.4 million. This is a lot less than the original NPV, calculated in Exhibit 5.14 to be $28 million! The method is more correct than the straight NPV approach above, but is a little more complex to use.[21] Note that the Productivity Index can also be calculated for purposes of effectively ranking projects, but this time using the ECV value as the numerator in Exhibit 5.15.

Scorecards

The notion here is that *qualitative factors,* such as leveraging core competencies and competitive advantage, are *much more important predictors of success* than are financial numbers, which are often in error. Many studies have probed new product success factors over the years, and there now exists a solid body of knowledge about which factors are the best predictors of new product success and profitability. A typical and proven list of scorecard criteria for valuating a new product project at the Go-to-Development decision point is shown in Exhibit 5.18.[22]

From this criteria list, an operational scorecard is created. This scorecard is then used at gate meetings by gatekeepers (senior management) to objectively evaluate and rate the project in question. The method has the added advantages of engaging senior management in the decision process in a structured and constructive way, adding some discipline to a potentially chaotic gate meeting, and ensuring that projects are objectively evaluated by an outside-the-team group of experienced people.

Effectiveness of these tools

For genuine new products, where there are greater unknowns, financial tools prove to be the least effective methods of selecting and ranking projects, according to a major Industrial Research Institute (IRI) study of portfolio methods and their efficacies.[23] This is due, not so much to the fact that the tool is unsound, but rather that the quality of data and projections – on expected sales, costs, and time to market – is so poor early in the life of a project, at the very time the key Go/Kill decisions must be made.

The scorecard method works, according to the IRI portfolio management study, although it is not the most popular method.[24] Scorecards are deemed an excellent tool for making early Go/Kill decisions on projects where financial information is limited and often unreliable; for example, at the first few gates in the case of genuine new product projects and platform developments. Thus, use the scorecard method – a much more qualitative method, but one that yields goods results – in conjunction with one or more of the financial tools above. Incidentally, best performers use two or more methods concurrently to select development projects; poorer performers tend to rely on a single tool.[25]

Exhibit 5.17 Determination of Expected Commercial Value of Project

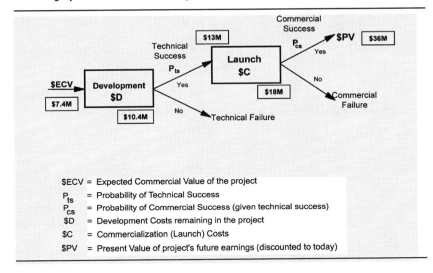

$ECV = Expected Commercial Value of the project

P_{ts} = Probability of Technical Success

P_{cs} = Probability of Commercial Success (given technical success)

$D = Development Costs remaining in the project

$C = Commercialization (Launch) Costs

$PV = Present Value of project's future earnings (discounted to today)

Exhibit 5.18 Best-In-Class Scoring Model for Product Innovation Projects — Gate 3

1. **Product Advantage:**
   - Unique product benefits to users
   - Differentiation vs. competitors' products
   - Meets customer needs better
   - Value for money

2. **Market Attractiveness:**
   - Market size
   - Market growth
   - Competitive situation

3. **Leverages Core Competencies:**
   - Marketing and distribution leverage

4. **Strategic:**
   - Alignment with Business's strategy
   - Strategic importance of project
   - Technological leverage
   - Manufacturing/Operations leverage

4. **Technical Feasibility:**
   - Size of technical gap
   - Technical complexity
   - Track record & technical uncertainty

5. **Risk Versus Return:**
   - Expected profitability (magnitude: NPV)
   - Return (IRR)
   - Payback period
   - Certainty of revenue, cost & profit estimates

- *Should Meet items (factors in bold) are scored (1-5 or 0-10) on a scorecard*
- *Factor scores must clear minimum hurdles*
- *Also added (weighted or unweighted) to yield Project Attractiveness Score*
  - *Compared to cut-off: Go/Kill*
  - *Used to rank projects: prioritization*

Resource Allocation to Specific Projects

Resource allocation is handled, in part, by the various project selection methods outlined above. For example, rank projects at a portfolio review until you run out of resources using the Productivity Index. If one is disciplined, the list of projects is just about right for the available resources. But the question of just who works on what projects remains a thorny one. Smaller and less sophisticated businesses handle the issue informally, often letting the project leader propose a list of candidates to work on his or her project. A step up is to use readily available and inexpensive software tools. Fortunately, rapid improvements in software automation tools have made resource allocation a much more manageable task in recent years. For example, *MS-Project*® is used as a planning tool by most project teams to map out the next steps of their project. But *MS-Project* can also be used to roll up the resource requirements from individual projects into resource requirements for the entire portfolio. Leading businesses increasingly rely on more advanced software also from Microsoft, such as the *Microsoft Office Enterprise Project Management solution (MS-EPM)*.[26] This software provides valuable tools to support the execution of the product development process, such as project scheduling, task-and-resource assignments, and time-and-task-completion tracking.

Using the Gates for Maximum Portfolio Productivity

Use your Go/Kill gates to scrutinize new product and development projects in depth. Gates are best held as a two-part meeting, as illustrated in Exhibit 5.19. The first part of the gate meeting (shown as the first diamond to the left in Exhibit 5.19) focuses strictly on the project in question. The deliverables and data are reviewed, and the question of whether or not the project is an attractive one is assessed.

We recommend that you employ financial tools at gates, in spite of their weaknesses, to assess project attractiveness; tools such as the NPV and ECV, as described above and in Exhibits 5.14 and 5.17. Consider using a financial approach that copes with risk, such as the risk-adjusted NPV or the ECV. In addition to financial tools, be sure to use the powerful and qualitative scorecard approach, again described above and in Exhibit 5.18. Questions in Part I of the gate are:

- Is the NPV positive? (calculate NPV using the appropriate risk-adjusted discount rate)
- Is the ECV positive? (ECV handles risk and probabilities)
- Does the IRR (internal rate of return as a percent) exceed your financial department's hurdle rate for this type of investment?
- And is the scorecard score greater than 65 out of 100?

If the answer is yes to all of the above questions, the project is judged to be an attractive one – it is a "Pass" as shown in Exhibit 5.19, but not necessary a Go. Note that gates are not only Go/Kill decision meetings; they are also *resource allocation meetings*, where resources must be assigned to the project and project team. Thus, gates must look beyond the individual project; the project must now be considered *in relation to all the other active and potential projects*. That's the second part of the gate meeting, shown as the second diamond in Exhibit 5.19.

Note: Be sure to be tough-minded at the gates, pruning out the weak projects. Exercising discipline at gate meetings and making real Kill decisions on weaker projects will greatly improve your product innovation productivity. You will get rid of low value projects but, most importantly, you will free resources to accelerate the higher value ones.

The major question is: Does the addition of this one project improve or do damage to the portfolio of development projects? Here the project's Productivity Index is compared to those of competing and active projects in the pipeline (as described in Exhibits 5.15 and 5.16). If the Productivity Index is higher than the portfolio average, then adding the new project will improve the overall Productivity Index of the portfolio.

Exhibit 5.19 Gates Are a Two-Part Decision

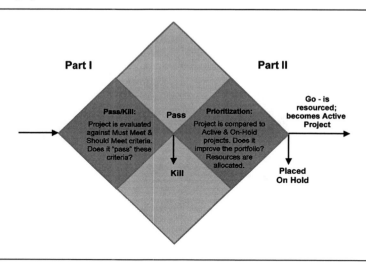

Exhibit 5.20 At Gates, Look at Impact On the Portfolio

☐ If you add this project to the Active List…
    ➢ Does it improve or reduce the value of your portfolio?
        · Use the Gate Scores & Productivity Indexes
        · Compare to other active projects

Project Name	Gate Score (0-10)	Productivity Index NPV/Person Days	Resources Required Loading (Person Days)	Sum of Loadings (Person Days)	Rank
Murray	8.3	206	120	120	1
Timor	8.3	194	140	260	2
Bering	7.5	180	90	350	3
Elk	7.8	142	180	530	4
Berlin	7.0	148	100	630	5

    ➢ Does this project require resources critical to (or employed on) other active projects?
        · Impact on other projects?
    ➢ Does this project help to balance the portfolio?
        · Or do you already have too many projects like this one?

(Use the project's scorecard score as well to compare it to other active projects.) We recommend that you also employ the prioritized list of projects in your gate meetings to show the comparisons and relative rankings, as illustrated in Exhibit 5.20.

Another equally difficult question concerns resources: If you do this one project, does it steal resources from another active project and slow it down? Or perhaps the project in question complements another project, making it easier to do? Finally, check your strategic buckets: Does the addition of this new project improve or worsen the balance in your portfolio? Use pie charts which portray spending breakdowns to date versus targets decided in your strategic buckets exercise, as shown in Exhibit 5.21. Then check what effect the addition of the new project would have on these pie charts: Does its addition bring you closer to your desired target of resource splits?

If the project passes the financial and scorecard hurdles and is deemed a positive addition to the portfolio – improves the overall Productivity Index, causes no serious resource conflicts and helps to balance the portfolio – then this is a strong project. The decision is Go and it is resourced. Move it forward!

Using the Portfolio Reviews for Maximum Portfolio Productivity

Portfolio reviews are also required to manage the entire portfolio of projects (bottom left of Exhibit 5.4). While the gates look at individual projects in depth, the portfolio review looks at *all development projects together*. Often this review, conducted by the same senior gatekeepers, is viewed as a sanity check or a minor course correction.

Here you use many of the same charts that are employed at gate meetings, as shown in Exhibit 5.22. Some of the portfolio checks and charts at the portfolio review are:

Exhibit 5.21 Check Balance and Buckets — Actual Versus Targeted Resource Allocation

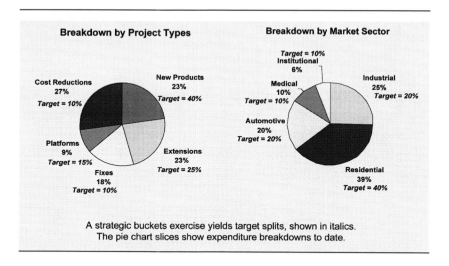

A strategic buckets exercise yields target splits, shown in italics.
The pie chart slices show expenditure breakdowns to date.

Exhibit 5.22 At Portfolio Reviews, Use Many of the Same Charts to Check for Prioritization, Balance and Alignment

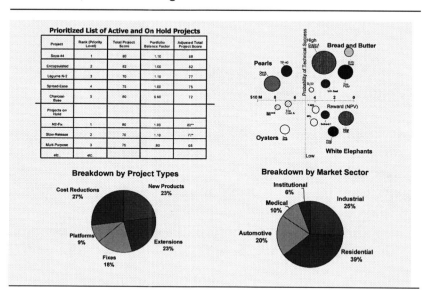

1. *Prioritized list of projects:* Perhaps the most useful chart is the prioritized list of active and on-hold projects in Exhibit 5.23. Here, you force rank all your projects within each bucket, one bucket at a time. Use the scorecard scores along with the Productivity Index to do this forced ranking. And be sure to show *project loadings* – the resources required in the next period (for the next quarter or next half-year) to undertake each project. The exercise here is to rank the projects and then add up the loadings or resource requirements until you run out of resources. Often this ranking exercise indicates that you have too many active projects in your portfolio and tough decisions must be made, such as putting some projects on hold. Other times, the exercise reveals that your original priorities and project rankings are wrong, and a re-prioritization of projects is called for.

2. *Sufficiency test:* Another solid check is the "sufficiency test". That is, ask the question: If you undertake all the "Go" projects in your active list in Exhibit 5.23, will your business achieve its product innovation goals? This involves estimating the sales or profits expected to be generated from each project, assigning a likelihood of the sales or profits occurring, and adding up the numbers.

3. *Strategic alignment:* You should also check for strategic alignment: Ensure that all your projects are strategically aligned and support your business's product innovation and technology strategy.

4. *Strategic buckets check:* Check for balance against your targets defined in your strategic buckets (the two pie charts at the bottom of Exhibit 5.22). Too many projects of one type or in one area may signal a need for a moratorium on future projects in that area.

5. *Risk profile:* Another useful chart is the risk-reward bubble diagram, as illustrated in Exhibit 5.24. Here the horizontal axis is some measure of the *reward* from each project and the vertical axis is a measure of *risk or probability of success.* The four-quadrants show the distribution

Exhibit 5.23 Look for the Right Prioritization of Active Projects

- ❑ Do you have the correct ranking?
- ❑ Are the right projects Active (versus on Hold)?

Project Name	Gate Score (0-10)	Stage	Productivity Index NPV/Person Days	Resources Required Loading (Person Days)	Sum of Loadings (Person Days)	Rank
Murray	8.3	3	206	120	120	1
Timor	8.3	4	194	140	260	2
Bering	7.5	3	180	90	350	3
Elk	7.8	2	142	180	530	4
Berlin	7.0	4	148	100	630	5
Columbia	8.0	Hold at Gate 3	150	120	-	hold
Snap	7.0	Hold at Gate 2	160	80	-	hold
Moose	7.5	Hold at Gate 2	108	130	-	hold
Banda	7.3	Hold at Gate 3	129	110	-	hold

Exhibit 5.24 Check for Balance and Risk Profile — Risk-Reward Bubble Diagram

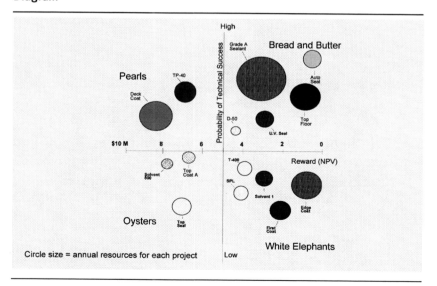

Circle size = annual resources for each project

of projects and resources (the size of the circles denotes resources going to each project), and the entire chart displays the risk vs. reward profile of your portfolio.

Conclusion

This completes the explanation of one of the most important – and certainly the most complex – principles of lean, rapid and profitable new product development: effective portfolio management. Major gains in productivity can be achieved through making more astute product innovation investment decisions, but few companies have implemented this principle well. There is much room for improvement. Consider putting a system in place that helps your business' leadership team make strategic portfolio decisions; for example, strategic buckets and product roadmaps. And then move to tactical decisions, using deliberate methods to rank, prioritize and select your development projects. Be sure to use several tools for this ranking, as a single method will not do the job.

Now, continue to the next chapter and witness the seventh and last principle: A flexible, adaptable, scalable and efficient idea-to-launch product innovation process – NexGen Stage-Gate® for accelerated product development projects.

CHAPTER 6

NexGen Stage-Gate®

A Flexible, Adaptive, Scalable and Efficient Product Innovation System – Principle Number 7

If You Don't Like the Results You're Getting . . .

If you don't like the results you're getting from product innovation, then look at the process or system that delivered them! Many companies are beginning to recognize that, although they have the rudiments of a product innovation process in place, it is anything but efficient and effective. In short, *their product innovation process is broken*: Projects take too long; key steps and activities are not done or done very well; rigorous gates are missing in the process; many projects circumvent the process altogether; and folks in the company generally see the existing product innovation process as a nuisance or bureaucratic. If these ailments sound familiar, read on, for what we present in this chapter is a look at the *next generation* or *next evolution* of the product innovation process.

A product innovation process, properly designed and implemented, works! The problem is that many senior management teams heard about the concept of a product innovation process some years ago, decided that

131

it was right for their business, but went about its design and implementation all wrong. And not surprisingly, the results are disappointing. A case of "the operation was a success but the patient died."

The fact is that high-productivity companies have got it right – they have overhauled and streamlined their idea-to-launch system, and it works! What steps have these companies taken to evolve their current product innovation process into the NexGen Stage-Gate system? First, they have *built in the first six principles* of *Lean, Rapid and Profitable NPD* we have presented in the last three chapters. Next they recognize that the "process" is more than just a process – it's really a *way of thinking and behaving* that must pervade the entire business. They have also made their process *scalable* – implemented different versions of the process tailored to different types and sizes of projects. And they have made their idea-to-launch system *flexible and adaptable*, with the process adjusting to different situations, circumstances and information.

Automation is becoming increasingly popular, as leading firms adopt and implement sophisticated software to help them drive their new products to market. We spend part of this chapter describing what *automation in product innovation* is and does so that you can better decide whether automated product innovation is right for your business. Also, in order to accelerate projects or take on more challenging projects, many companies look to co-development via *partnering and alliances*, and so Stage-Gate has evolved to handle these types of projects as well.

Finally, an emphasis on *lean methods* has resulted in much *waste removal in the process*, and the NexGen Stage-Gate is now much leaner, faster and more efficient. We reveal methods for identifying and eliminating non-value-added work in your current process. Improving the process and removing waste and inefficiencies to accelerate projects to market builds on Principle Number 5 in Chapter 4, metrics: accountability and continuous improvement.

Install a World-Class Idea-to-Launch Product Innovation Process

An idea-to-launch system for product innovation is one solution to what ails so many new product efforts.[1] Facing increased pressure to reduce the cycle time, yet improve their new product success rates, companies implement Stage-Gate systems to manage, direct, and control their product innovation initiatives (see an example of Stage-Gate in Exhibit 6.5). That is, these businesses have developed a systematic process – a playbook, game plan or framework – for moving a project through the various stages and steps from idea to launch.

Almost every best performing business has implemented a stage-and-gate system to drive new product projects through to commercialization, according to our benchmarking study. A solid idea-to-launch process is the most prevalent best practice observed among the sample of businesses, with almost 75 percent of businesses claiming to have such a process in place.[2] The PDMA's best practices study concurs: "Nearly 60 percent of the firms surveyed use some form of Stage-Gate process. Over half of the firms which have adopted Stage-Gate processes have moved from a basic process to more sophisticated versions with formal process ownership and facilitation (18.5 percent of the total) or third generation processes with more flexible gates and stage structures".[3] The most recent PDMA survey shows that 69 percent of businesses now have a cross-functional new product process in place.[4]

Claims and reality are somewhat different, however. While the great majority of businesses say that they have a stage-and-gate process in place, for many, it is a paper process or a process in name only. When we apply somewhat tougher criteria, such as "does the process have clearly defined stages? defined activities within stages? or defined gates with Go/Kill criteria?", many businesses miss the mark. Thus, we conclude that only about 54 percent of businesses really do have a legitimate new product process in place, as shown in Exhibit 6.1; but 71 percent of high-productivity businesses do – about twice as many as poor performers.[5]

**Exhibit 6.1 Highly Productive Businesses Practice the 7th Principle —
A Flexible, Adaptable, Scalable and Efficient Product Innovation Process**

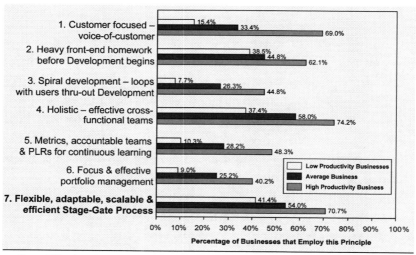

Source: CEK study, endnote 2.

What Stage-Gate Is

Imagine a product innovation machine, where you put your ideas in, and after the machine prioritizes and processes them, it delivers a steady stream of successful new products into the marketplace. Our machine sketched in Exhibit 6.2 epitomizes the ideal. In its simplest form, that's what Stage-Gate is – a product innovation machine! But Stage-Gate is a little more complicated than that!

Background

People often ask us: "How was Stage-Gate developed? It's so simple in concept, but so elegant and powerful once implemented… where did it come from?" Stage-Gate is the original new product process, and has become the standard methodology for product innovation in many companies around the world.[6] Stage-Gate has its roots in academic research. Beginning in the late 1970s, we observed and studied thousands of project teams in hundreds of different companies as they conceived, developed and launched new products. It was almost like watching video replays of football games on Monday morning, and analyzing the game play by play – what went wrong, what was done well, and so on. Most of this academic research was widely published in refereed and learned journals, hence stood the test of the peer review process.

Using the football analogy, after watching enough games, the coach finally takes out his own chalkboard and starts to map out how you will play the game – your own team's game plan or playbook. That's what we have done. Beginning in the early 1980s, the first versions of our new product process started to appear in test companies as a very crude and very early version of Stage-Gate. Since then, Stage-Gate has evolved to become a professional and world class system for driving new products to market used by leading companies worldwide. Stage-Gate is, thus, analogous to a playbook or game plan that a football team might use to drive the football from one end of the field down to the goal line and beyond – consistently, proficiently, quickly and game after game.

Later in this chapter, we'll share with you the latest evolution or version of Stage-Gate, which we label NexGen Stage-Gate. But for now, here is a quick review of what Stage-Gate is.

A Quick Primer on Stage-Gate

The Stage-Gate approach is a conceptual and operational model for moving a new product project from idea to launch.[7] It is a blueprint for managing the product innovation process to improve effectiveness and efficiency. Stage-Gate methods break the innovation process into a predetermined set of stages, each stage consisting of a set of prescribed, cross-functional and parallel activities, as shown in Exhibit 6.3. The entrance to each stage is a gate. These gates control the process and serve as the quality control and Go/Kill check points. This stage-and-gate format leads to the name "Stage-Gate" process.

Exhibit 6.2 The Structure and Content of Stage-Gate

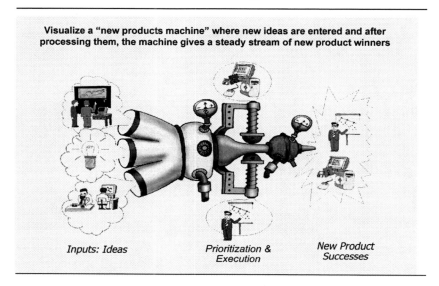

Visualize a "new products machine" where new ideas are entered and after processing them, the machine gives a steady stream of new product winners

Inputs: Ideas   Prioritization & Execution   New Product Successes

The stages

Stages are where the action occurs. They are analogous to the plays in a North American football game. The players on the project team undertake key tasks in order to gather information needed to advance the project to the next gate or decision-point.

Each stage begins at the exit of a gate, as shown in Exhibit 6.4 (this is analogous to exiting a huddle in a football game). The team begins each stage with an approved Forward Plan and approved resources (a check – for people and dollars – is cut at the gate). Also a date for the next gate is set, along with a list of required deliverables for the next gate – the expectations are clear.

The stages are defined by the activities within them, and there is usually a *fairly standard* or *prescribed list of actions* for each stage. This list includes both *recommended* and *mandatory* actions, designed to be undertaken in parallel. The activity list is based on best practices that are proven discriminators between best performers and the rest.

A closer look at the activities in a typical stage reveals that they are *information acquisition activities.* That is, the activities in each stage are designed to gather and yield the information needed to make excellent decisions at the next gate. Thus, the entire Stage-Gate system is designed as a risk management process. In order to manage risk, the parallel activities in each stage must be designed to gather vital information – technical, market, financial, operations – in order to drive down *both the technical and business risks* of the project. Each stage costs more than the preceding one, so that the game plan is based on incremental commitments. As uncertainties decrease, expenditures are allowed to mount, and risk is managed.

Throughout each stage, the emphasis is on quality of execution – doing it right – as well as rapid and efficient execution. The team also relies on sound project management methods, for example, using milestone and status meetings for updates and input, and keeping senior people engaged and informed.

Exhibit 6.3 Stages in the Stage-Gate System

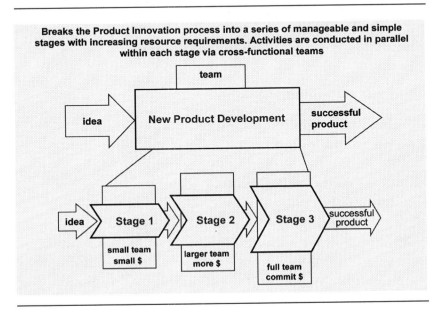

Exhibit 6.4 How Stages Work

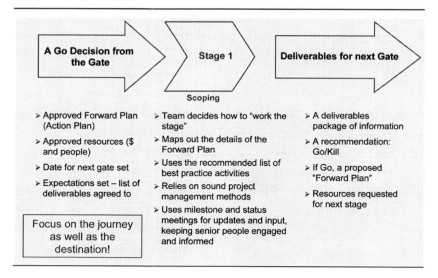

> - Approved Forward Plan (Action Plan)
> - Approved resources ($ and people)
> - Date for next gate set
> - Expectations set – list of deliverables agreed to

Focus on the journey as well as the destination!

> - Team decides how to "work the stage"
> - Maps out the details of the Forward Plan
> - Uses the recommended list of best practice activities
> - Relies on sound project management methods
> - Uses milestone and status meetings for updates and input, keeping senior people engaged and informed

> - A deliverables package of information
> - A recommendation: Go/Kill
> - If Go, a proposed "Forward Plan"
> - Resources requested for next stage

Stages are also cross-functional. There is no R&D or Marketing stage; rather, each stage consists of a set of parallel activities undertaken by *people from different functional areas* within the firm, working together as a team and led by a project team leader. And these actions within each stage occur rapidly and in parallel – a rugby approach.

The stages from idea-to-launch

The general flow of the typical Stage-Gate model is shown pictorially in Exhibit 6.5. The key stages are:

Stage 0 – Discovery: Pre-work designed to discover opportunities and to generate new product ideas.

Stage 1 – Scoping: A quick, preliminary investigation and scoping of the project. This stage provides inexpensive information – based largely on desk research – to enable the field of projects to be narrowed before Stage 2.

Stage 2 – Build the Business Case: A much more detailed investigation involving primary research – both market and technical – leading to a *business case.* This is where the bulk of the vital homework is done, and most of the market studies are carried out. The result is a business case that includes the product definition, the project justification, and a project plan.

Stage 3 – Development: The actual detailed design and development of the new product, along with some product testing work. The deliverable at the end of Stage 3 is an "alpha-tested" or "lab-tested product". Full production and market launch plans are also developed in this potentially lengthy stage.

Stage 4 – Testing and Validation: Tests or trials in the marketplace, lab, and plant to verify and validate the proposed new product, its marketing and manufacturing/production – field trails or beta tests; test market or trial sell; and operations/production trials.

Stage 5 – Launch: Commercialization and the beginning of full manufacturing or production, marketing, and selling. Here the market launch, production/operations, distribution, quality assurance and post-launch monitoring plans are executed.

At first glance, this overview portrays the stages as relatively simple steps in a logical process. But don't be fooled. What you see above is only a high level view of a generic process – the concept of the process. In a real company's process, drilling down into the details of each stage reveals a much more sophisticated and complex set of activities. Here you'll find a detailed list of activities within a stage, the how-to's of each activity, best practices that the project team ought to consider, and even the required deliverables from each activity in that stage (for example in the form of templates). In short, the drill-down provides a *detailed and operational playbook* for the project team – everything they need to know and do in order to successfully complete that stage of the process and project.

Exhibit 6.5 An Overview of NexGen Stage-Gate

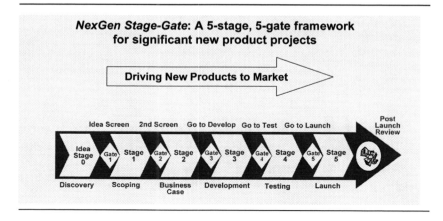

The gates

Preceding each stage is an entry gate or a Go/Kill decision point, shown as diamonds in Exhibit 6.6. The gates are the huddles on the football field. They are the points during the game where the team converges and where all new information is brought together. Gates are the decision points in the idea-to-launch framework – they ensure that only the right projects move forward.

Effective gates are central to the success of a fast-paced, product innovation process:

- Gates serve as quality control checkpoints: Is this project being executed in a quality fashion?
- Gates also serve as Go/Kill and prioritization decisions points: Gates provide the funnels, where mediocre projects are culled out at each successive gate.
- Finally, gates are where the action plan for the next stage is approved, along with resource commitments.

Exhibit 6.6 Gates in the Stage-Gate Framework

❑ **Each stage is preceded by a Gate – the diamonds**
❑ **Gates = Decision Points or Go / Kill Points**

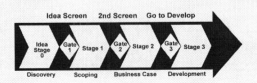

❑ **Gate are where projects get resources and are prioritized – get on senior management's radar screen**
❑ **Gates are the quality control check points in the process**

Exhibit 6.7 How Gates Work

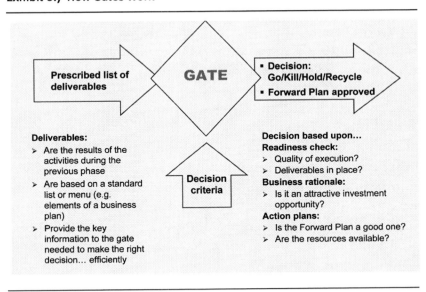

Gates have a common format, as shown in Exhibit 6.7:

1. *A set of required deliverables*: What the project leader and team must bring to the gate decision point (for example, the results of a set of completed activities). These deliverables are visible, are based on a standard menu for each gate, and are decided at the output of the previous gate. Management's expectations for project teams are made very clear.

2. Criteria against which the project is judged in order to make the Go/Kill and prioritization decisions (for example, the scorecards and financial criteria outlined in Chapter 5).

3. *Defined outputs*: a decision (Go/Kill/Hold/Recycle), an approved action plan for the next stage (complete with people required, money, person-days committed, and an agreed timeline), a list of deliverables, and a date for the next gate.

Gate meetings are usually staffed by senior managers from different functions – the gatekeepers – who *own the resources* required by the project leader and team for the next stage. Thus, the gatekeepers are usually the *leadership team of the business* for major projects at Gates 3, 4, 5 and the Post Launch Review (see Exhibit 6.5).

Building in Best Practices – Six of the LRP Principles

While many companies claim to have an idea-to-launch process, the best performers seem to get it right more often and build in more best practices. As seen in Chapters 2 to 5, high-productivity businesses embrace and practice the first six *Lean, Rapid and Profitable NPD principles* (Exhibit 6.1). That is, their product innovation process (or next generation Stage-Gate system) has evolved to incorporate these first six principles by design – they are part of the process, as illustrated in Exhibit 6.8. High-productivity businesses build in a strong customer focus into their Stage-Gate process and rely heavily on voice-of-customer research in the early days of their projects. They front-end load their projects, undertaking appropriate, often extensive up-front homework prior to

Development (by contrast, poor performers too often rush a poorly defined, poorly investigated project into Development, and suffer the consequences later!). And best performers focus on developing differentiated, superior products that meet customer needs better than their competitors. By contrast, poor performers tend to develop more undifferentiated, vanilla products with little competitive advantage.

In addition, high-productivity businesses emphasize a holistic approach and rely on truly cross-functional teams to drive new products to market. Their process includes project metrics built in, such as NPV, sales and on-time launch, so that performance results from individual projects can be gauged. Teams are accountable against these metrics, while continuous learning and improvement is very much part of the process – it is an *evergreen process*. Finally, high-productivity businesses have moved to effective portfolio management. They use strategic buckets and product roadmaps to help allocate development resources; and they build very tough Go/Kill decision points in the form of gates into their process (where mediocre projects really do get killed) complemented by portfolio reviews that ensure the total portfolio is strategically aligned and has the right number, mix and balance of projects.

Some of these activities and best practices in Exhibits 6.1 and 6.8 may seem self-evident and merely common sense. The problem is that they're not as common as one might think! Indeed, a quick look at Exhibit 6.1 reveals that only about one-third of companies on average employ each best practice. So take a hard look at your own idea-to-launch system, and critically assess whether the first six best-practice principles shown in Exhibit 6.1 are really built in. If they are not, build them in and you will have begun the transition to the NexGen Stage-Gate system.

Exhibit 6.8 First Six LRP Principles Built Into NexGen Stage-Gate

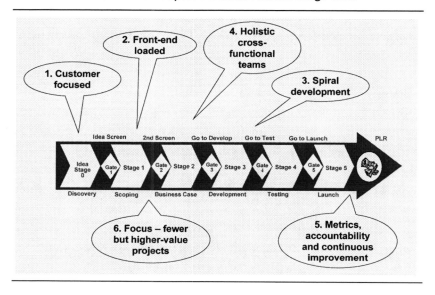

Key Features of the NexGen Stage-Gate System

A number of businesses have moved to next generation or NexGen Stage-Gate systems. They have incorporated techniques to render their product development efforts lean, rapid and profitable. Increased productivity in product innovation is the goal! Step one is to build in the first six principles outlined in Exhibit 6.1 and highlighted in Exhibit 6.8; but there are other worthwhile enhancements and changes to transition to the NexGen Stage-Gate system, which we outline now.

1. View Stage-Gate as a philosophy

Stage-Gate is more than a method or process. It is more than a set of flow charts, templates and check-lists. If that is all your process is to you, then you've missed most of the key benefits of Stage-Gate! The best companies now see their product innovation process as a *philosophy or culture that fosters new and desired behavior.* Success in product innovation requires many behavioral changes, such as discipline; deliberate, fact-based and transparent decision-making; responsible, accountable, effective and truly cross-functional teams; continuous improvement and learning from mistakes; and risk taking and risk awareness. The structure and content of the NexGen Stage-Gate process must be viewed as a *vehicle for change* – for changing the way people think, act, decide and work together.

Some action implications of this philosophical and behavioral perspective of Stage-Gate are the following:

Training: Many businesses underestimate the behavioral changes required of project teams and gatekeepers when they implement Stage-Gate. By contrast, the best performers conduct considerable training when they install their product innovation process. For example, Exxon Chemical trained over one thousand people when it first implemented its Product Innovation Process.[8] ITT Industries trained hundreds of new product practitioners in dozens of business units when its Value Based Product Development process went live. Procter & Gamble is currently focusing on the training of project team leaders. The point is that installing a NexGen Stage-Gate process requires project team members to undertake activities and tasks that they may not be familiar with or trained to do; for example, the voice-of-customer work and the spiral development approach outlined in Chapter 3, or the use of metrics and continuous improvement in Chapter 4. The goal is to get project team members to really practice the first six principles of NexGen Stage-Gate. Do not assume that they will do so by default – some rigorous training is probably required.

Training is not only directed at project team members and leaders, but at gatekeepers as well. Indeed the greatest change of behavior is usually at the gatekeeper level. Thus, some firms have implemented what amounts to "gatekeeper boot camp" to try to effect the needed behavioral changes in the senior leadership team of the business.

Rules of engagement: Any team sport requires rules of play, conduct or engagement. Stage-Gate is no different. When gatekeepers consistently miss gate meetings, arrive unprepared, do not use the agreed-to gate criteria, fail to make clear and timely Go/Kill decisions, or fail to commit the needed resources to projects, it is time to develop and agree to a set of "gatekeeper rules of engagement" – a codebook by which the gatekeepers live. We find that individual gatekeepers are well aware that some of their colleagues' behavior is detrimental to the effective use of a Stage-Gate system, but often are reluctant to point this out. A frank and open session on developing gatekeeper rules of engagement is the vehicle to air these concerns and to develop a code of conduct.

Defined roles and responsibilities of team members: Other behavioral and attitude changes occur in terms of the roles and responsibilities of project team members. Many of these desired behaviors have been outlined in Principle Number 4 – holistic, cross-functional teams – and Principle Number 5 – accountable cross-functional teams and continuous improvement. But these behaviors need to be constantly reinforced, including simple tenets such as:

- The project team members work as an entrepreneurial team, much like a business start up. They think for themselves, propose forward plans, and do not wait to be led or directed by their bosses.
- The entire team, not just a few players, is accountable for the end result and not for just one facet of the project.
- Winning in the marketplace is the goal, not just getting one's project through the next gate review. Success criteria must be established as part of the business case, and the team is held accountable for achieving results against these criteria.
- When problems are identified, focus on preventing their recurrence – go to the root cause.
- On exiting a gate meeting, the Go/Kill decision must be made; it must be clear, and it must be communicated to all who need to know the outcome or decision. In the event of a Go decision, expectations

regarding what the team will do next and what they will deliver at the next gate must be agreed to and clear to everyone.

These and other behavioral changes should be part of your NexGen Stage-Gate system. Don't forget the "people side" or behavioral facets of the game!

2. Make your Stage-Gate scalable

NexGen Stage-Gate is flexible and adjustable by scale, nature, magnitude and risk level of different development project types. It suits all types of new products, including service developments as well as physical products, or any combination of these. There is no longer just one version of Stage-Gate. Rather the process has *morphed into multiple versions.* Exhibit 6.9 shows some examples: Stage-Gate *XPress* for projects of moderate risk, such as improvements, modifications and extensions; Stage-Gate *Lite* for very small projects, such as simple customer requests. And there is even Stage-Gate TD for technology development projects, where the deliverable is new knowledge, new science or a new technological capability.[6]

The principle for choosing which version of Stage-Gate to use for product development is simple: The higher the risk, the more one adheres to the standard model or full five-stage process as laid out in Exhibit 6.5. But what is risk in product innovation? Risk has two major components:
1. What is at stake, such as:
   • the total costs to undertake the project
   • the potential payoffs – the "size of the prize"
   • the strategic impact and importance of the project.
2. Uncertainty:
   • how new or step-out the project is
   • how many unknowns lie in the path ahead.

Based on this definition of risk, different project types are evident in product innovation, and clearly your Stage-Gate system must be adapted or scaled to accommodate each type. For example, product development project types might be categorized into these three types, as shown in Exhibit 6.10:

1. Genuine new products can be:
   - A new product offering for the business (and can be totally new to the market too – an innovation).
   - A market-based product with multiple target customers.
   - New features, functionality or benefits to the customer or user that are clearly visible to the customer or user.
   - A significant development effort, for example: at least 125 person-days, one-half person-year, or the out-sourced equivalent.

These are higher risk new product projects and thus employ the full five-stage process shown at the top of Exhibit 6.9.

Exhibit 6.9 NexGen Stage-Gate Is Scalable

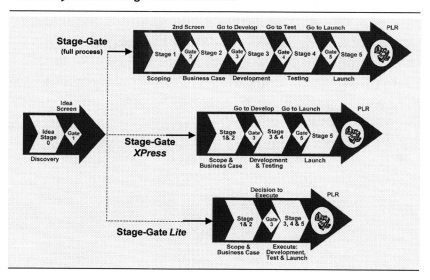

Exhibit 6.10 Stage-Gate for Three Different Types of New Product Projects

Project Type	Characteristics	Process Type
Genuine new products	New product offering for the business with multiple target customers (can be new to the market – an innovation). Product has new features, functionality or benefits visible to the customer or user.	**Use the full or regular 5-stage Stage-Gate Process (top, Exhibit 6.9)**
Improvements, modification & extensions	A visible modification to an existing company product. Multiple target customers (more than a single customer). A sustaining innovation.	**Use the 3-stage Stage-Gate *XPress* (middle, Exhibit 6.9)**
Marketing or Sales request	A single customer request. A minor modification to an existing product. (Done at low cost and no capital cost)	**Use the 2-stage Stage-Gate *Lite* (bottom, Exhibit 6.9)**

2. Improvements, modification and extensions:
   - A visible improvement, modification or extension of an existing company product
   - Multiple target customers
   - A product needed to sustain the business – a sustaining innovation
   - A moderate Development effort; for example, at least 40 person-days of development effort (or two person-months).

These improvements, modifications and extensions are somewhat lower risk – they usually cost less to do and involve fewer unknowns (as they are based on an existing company product), but they still consume resources, and deliberate decisions must be made on them. Use the three-stage process or Stage-Gate *XPress* shown across the middle of Exhibit 6.9.

3. A Marketing or Sales request:
   - A single customer request
   - A minor modification to an existing product
   - Usually done at low cost.

These projects, requested from Marketing or the Salesforce, are usually the lowest risk as they involve little effort and are a minor modification to an existing product. Here we recommend that you employ a two-stage process or Stage-Gate *Lite* as shown across the bottom of Exhibit 6.9. Individually these small projects require few resources; but without discipline, collectively they can eat up almost all your resources. So they do require deliberate Go/Kill decisions (top performers do not do all of these projects regardless) and they also require some discipline in their execution. That is, don't let these "small projects" circumvent the system.

Note: In Exhibit 6.9, all development projects enter Gate 1 on the left for an initial screen. Gate 1 is in effect a "clearing house". The idea screening decision is made here, as is the routing decision – what type of project this is, and therefore what process or system it should be in.

There are other development projects that are not new products in the strictest sense, but nonetheless do compete for the same resources. Exhibit 6.11 provides a list of some of these project types. You may also wish to handle these projects in a similar gating fashion, each with its own version of a Stage-Gate system (modified versions of those systems in Exhibit 6.9). Other project types, such as technology and platform developments, will require a special Stage-Gate system.[10]

3. Make your Stage-Gate system adaptable and flexible

The notion of a rigid, lock-stepped process is dead! Rather, today's fast-paced NexGen Stage-Gate system is *adaptable and flexible*. No activity is mandatory, nor is every deliverable required for every project – the suggested list in each stage is much like a menu from which to choose. Those activities that the team elects to do should depend on the nature and needs of each project. The system, thus, allows the project team *considerable latitude in deciding what actions are needed in their project* and what deliverables are appropriate for each gate. That is, the team decides how to "work the stage" and maps out the details of their plan of action for the stage, deciding what deliverables they will deliver to the next gate (subject to approval of Gatekeepers at previous gate).

The system is also adaptable to fluid and dynamic information. The concept of *spiral development* – building in a series of "build-test-feedback and revise" loops or spirals from the early days of the project all the way

Exhibit 6.11 Other Types of Development Projects That Use Stage-Gate

Project Type	Characteristics	System or Process
Cost Reduction	A product redesign to remove product cost. Usually a smaller, lower risk project with no visible product/performance change for the user	Use a process similar to Stage-Gate *XPress* or *Lite*. Integrate with your Six Sigma process.
Outsourced Project	A new product but with Development work done by others. Project can be any size, and as a result, can be risky (but it is a shared risk)	Use a process similar to one of three processes in Exhibit 6.9, depending on risk.
Repositioning	The same product but with a new application. Usually minimal technical work is involved. Considerable marketing and applications work maybe required	Use Stage-Gate *XPress* or *Lite*, with some technical activities deleted.
Platform Development	The development of a new capability or a "launching platform" for multiple new products. Can be huge, high impact and very risky with many unknowns	Use a special version of Stage-Gate (endnote 9).
Technology Development	Deliverable is new knowledge or a new technological capability. Has many technical unknowns and uncertainties. May ultimately spawn multiple new products	Use a special version of Stage-Gate (endnote 9).
Process Development	The "deliverable" is a new or improved manufacturing process. Can be huge and risky, or small and inexpensive. May overlap with Platform or Technology Developments (above)	Use a different version of Stage-Gate. Similar in principle to New Product Process, but different activities & criteria. Can be 2-, 3- or 5-stages.

through to field trials – is one way that fast-paced project teams cope with changing, fluid information and, at the same time, get their product definition right. Exhibit 3.13 in Chapter 3 showed a sample series of loops or iterations, beginning early in Stage 2 with voice-of-customer research followed quickly by a full proposition concept test using, for example, a virtual prototype and a simulated selling presentation. Similar fast-paced iterations or spirals continue through the Development stage and right up to pre-Launch.

Further, in a flexible Stage-Gate system, activities can overlap, with the principle of *simultaneous execution* employed – not waiting for the total completion of a previous step and 100 percent perfect information before moving ahead, as outlined in Chapter 3. The system is not a relay race, with every activity done sequentially and linearly. Rather, the process is more like a rugby game, with multiple activities done concurrently and overlapping each other.

The Cost of Delay

Calculating the cost of delay in a project is a powerful tool that drives home the point – why acceleration and a time-emphasis are so critical. It also helps to justify, on a rational and economic basis, why certain activities should be deleted or modified and why your procedures need to be changed based upon your map of the value stream analysis.

The cost of delay can be computed on a per-working-day basis. It includes the following elements:

1. **The cost of the deferred income stream:** Money has a time value! Determine your cash profit stream or stream of future earnings after Launch. Then determine the present value (PV in $000) of this income stream, and multiply by your cost of capital per day (%). That's how much deferring your new product's income by one day costs you!

2. **The lost window of opportunity:** If your product has a limited window of opportunity in which to generate sales (many products do), then determine the cost of these lost sales (on a per day basis). Note that these are early life-cycle sales, when prices and margins are likely to be higher. Products that are seasonal or needed for a key selling season or trade show often have huge costs of delay.

3. **The extra development costs:** Any project that lasts longer invariably ends up costing more than it should. Try to impute an extra cost per day here (this will usually be less than the total Development per day).

4. **Loss of competitive advantage:** In fast moving and competitive markets, where being first in really matters, the costs of delay might also include a penalty for losing out to a competitor – for losing the "first in position".

5. **Other costs:** On occasion, other costs of delay are incurred, and should be included. Examples are: the costs of delivering late to a key customer (sometimes there are contractual penalties) or of delaying a partner's launch of their product.

Calculate the cost of delay on a per-day basis. For every day you postpone or delay the project, this is what it costs your business. Use the Cost of Delay calculation in your value stream mapping, your Post Launch Review, and also when mapping out a new product for the first time.

Example: At Toyota, effective concurrent engineering requires that each subsequent function maximize the utility of the stable information available from the previous function as it becomes available.[11]

Recall Exhibit 3.10 (the four-quadrant information diagram) that helps to define when to move forward. The rule is this: Move forward and base your decisions on stable and reliable information. A word of caution, however: Overlapping activities and moving forward on the basis of early, unreliable and fluid data will result in much waste, according to experts at Toyota.[12] You think you are saving time, but you will actually take longer than in a linear process.

Another rule: Overlap the activities from one stage into the previous stage. For example, one does not wait for formal launch-gate approval to move into some facets of the final stage (the Launch stage in Exhibit 6.5). Rather, long lead-time launch activities – such as salesforce training, preparation of marketing collaterals, and ordering raw materials – can be moved forward into the previous stage (into the Testing stage in Exhibit 6.5) in order to accelerate the project, *even though the project has not yet been approved for Launch, and may yet be cancelled at Gate 5.* Here the project team weighs the cost of delay versus the costs incurred by moving activities forward in the event the project is cancelled (along with the likelihood of cancellation occurring). That is, the project team justifies accelerating activities (or moving activities forward) based on a quantitative assessment of:

- The cost of delay: the number of days that will be saved multiplied-by the cost-per-day of delaying the project (see box entitled *The Cost of Delay*)
- The cost of being wrong: the loss incurred if the project is indeed cancelled (for example, wasted promotional materials work) multiplied-by the probability that the project will be cancelled.

4. Automate your product innovation process

Progressive companies recognize that automation greatly enhances the effectiveness of their product innovation process.[13] Although many companies have attempted to implement a solid idea-to-launch process, often a business struggles with adoption. This is because, too often, the processes they have put in place are administratively burdensome and difficult-to-use.

One increasingly popular way of enabling process adoption and adherence is the use of automation software. The benefits of automation are two-fold: Less time is required to complete process activities and deliverables; and the administrative task-load associated with process execution is dramatically reduced. For example, project team members can more easily create gate deliverables, search for documents, and perform other routine tasks because they have ready access to embedded templates and best-practice content. Some automation systems pre-populate templates for key deliverables (such as status reports, presentations, and resource charts) with project information that has been recorded elsewhere in the system. As a result, documents and other materials that previously took hours or days to prepare can be completed in minutes. The templates further serve as how-to references that project team members follow as they complete tasks, helping to ensure that key process steps are followed. Automation can also help project leaders by providing them with pre-formatted models for the creation of new projects, including definitions for each stage and gate and listings of corresponding deliverables. Such pre-formatted models also help to ensure consistency in process execution.

Another benefit associated with process automation is the streamlining of communications and knowledge-sharing among project team members and with gatekeepers or executives. Everyone from project team member to senior executive has access to the right view of relevant information – the information that they need to move their project forward, to cooperate with other team members globally on vital tasks, or to help make the Go/Kill decision. By allowing critical project information to be stored in one central location, automation makes it possible for the Stage-Gate process manager or project leader to assign and track tasks on-line across multiple innovation projects. As team members complete tasks, they can share deliverables, work on them collaboratively and communicate status reports immediately. This greatly simplifies the project reporting process for the project leader.

Automation also gives executives the ability to view all the active projects in their innovation portfolio at a glance and to drill down into the details of individual projects. For example, many of the automation systems have extensive built-in portfolio management tools, complete with the portfolio displays like those outlined in Chapter 5. These displays are generated automatically from the software database. Having access to this information allows executives to spot at-risk projects, to rank projects (for example, according to such criteria as NPV, the productivity index, or the project score, or any other stored parameter or characteristic of projects), or to determine the impact of shifts in resource allocations and project priorities on the product innovation portfolio.

In order to realize the benefits of information access, decision-support systems and time-savings, automation software tools, such as *Accolade*® by Sopheon, are increasingly being adopted by leading businesses and must be considered part of the NexGen Stage-Gate system.[14] For example, *Accolade* integrates strategy, portfolio management, *Stage-Gate*® and idea management – a business decision support system for making innovation investment decisions more effectively and efficiently.

Additionally, standard off-the-shelf versions of Stage-Gate – a "stage-gate-process-in-a-box" – and web-based versions, also exist. These Stage-Gate tools, although not automation per se, facilitate the implementation and use of an idea-to-launch process. They can be quickly adapted and implemented in your business (see for example *SG-Navigator*[TM] in endnote 15).

5. Adapt your process for partnering and alliance projects

Much evidence exists to suggest that co-development, via partnering or alliances, is more successful for some types of development projects.[16] Partnering with customers, for example, can reduce market risk, provide better customer insights, yield instant customer feedback, facilitate development spirals, and accelerate launch and product adoption. Partnering with a technology partner can reduce technical risk, improve the odds of technical success, reduce development costs and time, and may even make an otherwise non-feasible project quite attractive for the business. Thus, much of your product innovation effort should involve partners, alliances and out-sourced vendors.

Increasingly leading firms are building a *co-development sub-process* into their regular product innovation process to handle these partnerships or two-party projects. Embedded within the stages of the NexGen Stage-Gate process are key external activities, such as identifying the need for partners, seeking potential partners, and vetting candidate partners. And gate criteria are also built in for partnering issues, for example evaluating a project with and without a partner in place.

Sometimes a partner is identified right at the beginning of the project – for example, a traditional alliance partner you work with may come to you with the new product idea. Alternatively, the need for a partner often arises as part of your project investigation work. Both scenarios should be handled by your product innovation process. Here are some of the additions that are often built into your NexGen Stage-Gate system to accommodate the partnering situation:

Discovery: Ideas and partnering proposals from potential-partner companies are welcomed into your idea handling and screening system. A Go/Kill decision is made based on criteria that assume the presence of a partner, and the decision at Gate 1 is communicated to the partner. Legal and intellectual property (IP) issues are identified and a preliminary legal/IP strategy is mapped out.

Scoping: If a partner has already been identified, your Stage 1 preliminary investigation team meets with and maps out Stage 1 activities. Legal and IP issues must be resolved. A letter of intent for the project is proposed and signed.

The two teams – yours and the partner's – work in parallel and cooperatively. They share the Stage 1 work-load and information; and they may even develop a joint package of Gate 2 deliverables. Gate 2 may be a joint gate meeting between the two companies.

If no partner has been identified at this point, Stage 1 involves the identification of the need for a partner (for example, consider what your voids, gaps and deficiencies are in terms of making the project a success; Thus, what skills, resources and experience the ideal partner should have). A preliminary scouting for possible partners is undertaken. The pros and cons of transforming the project into a co-development project are identified and are part of the preliminary business case delivered to Gate 2.

Build the Business Case: If a partnership is in place, the two project teams work cooperatively, mapping out their respective forward plans. Market, technical and business assessments are undertaken cooperatively. For example, voice-of-customer interviews and concept testing may be done with team members from both companies visiting customers together as part of the interview team. Gate 3 may be a joint gate meeting.

If no partner has been formally designated at this point, Stage 2 involves a much more thorough investigation of possible partners, and a rigorous vetting of potential partners – their resources, skills and experience and what they bring to the table. A recommended partner is defined as part of the Gate 3 business case, along with a non-binding memorandum of understanding between the two firms. The expectation is that both parties have done some due diligence work here, and understand what is required to make this alliance project successful. Legal and IP issues must be identified and a legal/IP strategy mapped out.

Gate 3 may be a joint gate meeting with the partner's executives attending as well, although issues regarding the choice of the partner should be discussed previously and privately. The outcome of the gate meeting, where the project is approved, is often a letter of intent with some legal obligations and commitments. Note, however, that the project may yet be cancelled at subsequent gates.

Development: The actual detailed design and development of the new product proceeds with both project teams – the one from your company and the partner's – working hand-in-hand. Rigorous project management methods must be in place in both firms, and the team leaders meet regularly to review progress and deal with challenges. Limited customer tests and various spirals undertaken with the customer also proceed cooperatively. Finally, full production and market launch plans are developed jointly by the two teams.

Testing and Validation: The two teams continue to work together, conducting tests or trials in the marketplace, lab, and plant to verify and validate the proposed new product, and its marketing and operations. The joint Launch plans are finalized between the two companies.

Launch: Here the integrated or joint market launch, operations, distribution, quality assurance and post-launch monitoring plans are executed. The project teams from both companies may expand with the addition of commercial people, such as sales and operations. The Post Launch Review may be a joint meeting with representatives from both companies attending.

Experience dictates that if both companies possess a well-articulated and proficient idea-to-launch process or Stage-Gate system, then working together is greatly facilitated. Where only one business has such a process, often it is difficult to track the project – for example, determining just where the project is in the partner firm, and whether or not key activities are actually happening, or being overlooked, or stalled. Thus, one of the first activities the project or executive team might face is to help your partner install a product innovation process!

6. Remove all waste in your process – make it lean

Borrow the concepts from *lean manufacturing* and apply them to your product innovation process in order to remove waste in the process. By analyzing a map of the idea-to-launch *value stream*, all non-value-added items are removed. A value stream is simply the connection of all the process steps with the goal of maximizing customer value.[17] In product innovation, a value stream represents the linkage of all value-added and non-value-added activities associated with the creation of a new product or service. The tool known as the *value stream map* is used to identify and document value streams, and is critical to identifying both value-added and non-value-added activities, hence it is an essential tool to improving your idea-to-launch or Stage-Gate process.[18]

Here are several approaches to developing and using a value stream map:

1. *The value stream map for your typical product development project:* Create a map of the value stream for typical product development projects in your business, that is, a map of your current idea-to-launch process. Map out all the stages, decision-points and key activities in a typical project. Be sure to indicate typical times for each activity and decision. This work is usually done by a task force comprised of experienced project team leaders and team members. Note that there is often a difference between the way the process is supposed to work, and the way it actually works in reality!

In this exercise, consider mapping different types of typical projects: a major product development, an extension or a modification, and a customer request project. Do this as a team or task force, using a long roll of paper on a wall. An example of a map of a value stream is shown in Exhibit 6.12, with typical times shown for each key activity in the process.

Once the value stream or process is mapped out, lower the microscope on the process and dissect it. Critically assess each step and activity in the process, and pose six key questions:

- What work gets done at this step, stage or activity?
- How long does it typically take?
- How well do you execute (rate the quality of execution: 0-10)?
- Is this step or activity really needed?
- If it is, how can it be made better?
- How can it be made faster?

Examine all procedures, required deliverables, documents and templates, meetings and decision processes in your current idea-to-launch process. Look for time wasters and "speed bumps". Be sure to determine the cost of delay and specifically how much each delay costs you in dollars (see box entitled The Cost of Delay).

Once problems, time-wasters and non-value-added activities are identified, then the task force works to remove them. Consider using a Six Sigma approach to focus on solving persistent problems with your process. The goal is to revise, improve and overhaul your product innovation process and to translate it into a much leaner and more efficient NexGen Stage-Gate system.

2. Post Launch Reviews on recently completed projects: Continuous learning and improvement is a key facet of the lean method, with post-mortems undertaken at the Post Launch Review to provide insights on how to do projects better and faster (the Post Launch Review or PLR in Exhibits 6.5 and 6.9). The result is a much more efficient and effective idea-to-launch method. So be sure to conduct a retrospective analysis of past projects at your Post Launch Review. (Some companies even undertake a similar analysis at each gate review for larger projects!). Recall from Chapter 4 that high-productivity businesses build in continuous learning and improvement, and the retrospective analysis is a key component of this learning.

The methodology employed was outlined in Chapter 4 and is in fact very similar to the value stream mapping exercise outlined above (except that it is conducted on recently-completed projects). The exercise focuses on root cause counter-measures to stop future recurrence of problems and

Exhibit 6.12 Value Stream Map for the Stage-Gate Process

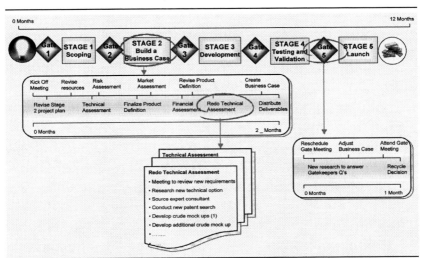

time delays. The goal is always the same: Continuous learning, namely learning how to do the next project better and faster.

3. Flow-charting every new project: Upon exiting each gate, the project team has resources, the next-gate's deliverables defined, and a high level forward plan approved. As the next stage begins, new team members are often added to the team, and the forward plan needs to be fleshed out in much more detail. At this point, smart team leaders engage the entire team (including the new team members) in an effective team-building exercise: mapping out the detailed action plan for the stage. This exercise kills three birds with one stone: First, it's a valuable way to *build the team*, to introduce the new team members, and to integrate them into the project quickly. Second, it yields a much sharper and robust action plan, complete with *realistic timelines*, much better than the project leader developing the action plan on his or her own, or each team member developing their own piece of the plan independently. Finally, because this is a team exercise, it becomes the *team's action plan*, not just the plan developed by the project leader – there is greater buy-in and ownership.

A useful addition to this exercise – and one which greatly improves the action plan – is to encourage the team to do a detailed walk-through of the project. In short, once the action plan is mapped out, go through the action plan for the next stage in detail – step by step, activity by activity – and ask the same questions you might ask in a Post Launch Review:

- How could you do the project better?
- How could you do it faster?

The main difference is that these are forward-looking questions rather than asked retrospectively, and they are posed early enough so the team can still take corrective action. When undertaking this exercise, be sure to consider the cost of delay – what the cost per day is for each day the project is late.

The team should also map out a tentative or throw-away plan right through to Launch. The details of this plan are obviously very tentative, but even here, steps can be taken to anticipate long lead-time activities and time-consuming tasks, so that accelerated or preventive actions can be taken early.

Conclusion

The NexGen Stage-Gate system represents the next evolution in product innovation processes. NexGen Stage-Gate is the integration and embodiment of all the seven principles of *Lean, Rapid and Profitable New Product Development*. It is the key to improving your NPD productivity.

The first step, of course, is to ensure that your business has embraced and implemented the first six principles, as summarized in Exhibit 6.13. But the leap – and the real challenge – is the total integration of these principles into your NexGen Stage-Gate system and then *living the process* – making it a way of life in your business. And don't forget the added features highlighted in this chapter, namely:

- Viewing your system less as a process and more as a philosophy – way of thinking and behaving.
- Making your process scalable in order to accommodate the different types and sizes of projects that you undertake.
- Building in flexibility and making the process adaptive – flexible activities and deliverables; simultaneous execution; and overlapping stages and activities.
- Automating your product innovation process.
- Ensuring that your process accommodates partnership and alliance projects.
- And, most importantly, removing the waste and inefficiencies in your value stream or process – making it a lean process.

Only a handful of companies worldwide have managed to evolve their innovation processes to this level, building in all seven principles including those facets outlined in this chapter. But most high-productivity businesses have implemented some or the majority of the seven principles, (as seen in Exhibit 6.1), and are reaping the benefits. Review the list in Exhibit 6.13, and review the ingredients of the NexGen Stage-Gate system in this chapter. Then make a commitment to move forward – Lean, Rapidly and Productively!

Exhibit 6.13 The Seven Principles of Lean, Rapid and Profitable NPD

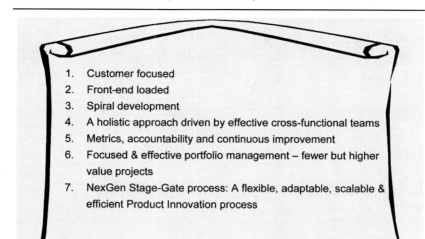

1. Customer focused
2. Front-end loaded
3. Spiral development
4. A holistic approach driven by effective cross-functional teams
5. Metrics, accountability and continuous improvement
6. Focused & effective portfolio management – fewer but higher value projects
7. NexGen Stage-Gate process: A flexible, adaptable, scalable & efficient Product Innovation process

Implementing The Seven Principles

A Quick Walk Through the Seven Principles of Lean, Rapid and Profitable New Product Development

Many best practices have been outlined in this book. Each one has been found, in at least several research studies, to impact very positively on product innovation performance, and all seven are identified in our most recent benchmarking study to be significantly correlated with NPD productivity.[1] At first glance, the list of best practices may be overwhelming to you, but when you break the practices down and integrate the list into Seven Principles, it is quite manageable. So let's walk through the Seven Principles and be sure that each is understood by you and your senior management team. As we begin, think about whether each principle is right for you, and then about how to implement it – how to move forward and put each principle in place.

1. Customer focused

The first goal is developing and delivering new products that are differentiated, solve major customer problems, and offer a compelling *value proposition* to the customer or user. This is the number one key to success and profitability at the project level. Begin with a thorough understanding of the customers' and users' unmet and unarticulated needs. This is achieved mostly through in-depth and in-the-field voice-of-customer work. And don't let others in your organization – the salesforce or product manager – speak for the customer or user. Instead, demand that the project team touch real customers! This voice-of-customer work should begin early; for example, in the Discovery stage of your Stage-Gate process, to seek out excellent ideas. And this customer work is certainly part of Stage 2, Build Business Case, where the fledgling product concept is translated into a robust and winning product definition. The customer or user should be an integral part of the entire development process from discovery through to product definition, development and right to validation and beyond.

2. Front-end loaded

Don't skip over the front-end work on new product projects! A good dose of the right up-front homework pays for itself ten-fold in terms of saving time and higher success rates. Build in the right front-end homework on projects – the right market, technical and business assessments – into Stages 1 and 2 of your Stage-Gate system. You saw examples of what this front-end work looks like in Chapter 3 – the eight key actions culminating in a product definition and Business Case. And demand that the front-end work be done – that project teams really understand that this homework makes the difference between winning and losing, and that it must be undertaken! This homework should not be excessive: It is designed to yield just enough of the vital information to make a Gate 3 Go-to-Development decision, and to define the product and project sufficiently to proceed. The right homework is also instrumental to yielding a winning product and project definition.

3. Spiral development

Practice *spiral development*. That is, build in a series of iterative steps or loops – "build-test-feedback and revise" spirals – into your Stage-Gate system. Develop a first version of the product, such as a virtual prototype very early, perhaps in Stage 2. Then test this concept with the customer or user, seeking feedback. Use the feedback to produce the next and more complete version, perhaps a working model or protocept early in Stage 3, Development, and so on. Remember that people don't know what they're looking for until they have seen it, or have experienced it! So get successive iterations in front of the customer or user often and early. Encourage your project teams to remove unnecessary work and to move quickly to a finalized product by building this series of iterative loops into their project plan from scoping right through the development phase and into testing.

4. A holistic approach driven by effective cross-functional teams

The core team – an effective cross-functional project team – is the number one key to cycle time reduction and to getting to market on time. Build your Stage-Gate system on effective cross-functional teams comprised of players drawn from different parts of the organization, each with an equal stake in and commitment to the project. The team is entrepreneurial and functions like a business start-up, proposing plans and solutions, and not waiting to be led by their bosses. Team players should remain on the project from end to end, not just for one stage of the project. And projects should be led by a clearly defined and carefully selected team leader from any function, who also remains on the project from end to end. Finally the team and leader must be given some power and authority over the project, resources and assigned people's time. In return, they are accountable for the project's commercial results measured against success criteria at the Post Launch Review.

5. Metrics, accountability and continuous improvement

You can't manage what you don't measure, so put metrics in place. Measure how well your business is doing at product innovation, and hold the business leadership team accountable for results. Most importantly, measure how well individual projects perform by building a Post Launch Review as well as gate reviews into your Stage-Gate system. Here, project teams are held accountable for delivering promised results against these metrics. And when gaps, problems and weaknesses are identified, hold problem solving sessions that focus on root causes so that corrective actions designed to stop future recurrence are identified. Thus, learning and continuous improvement become an integral and routine facet of your Stage-Gate system – "every project executed better than the one before". Your Stage-Gate system must be an *evergreen process*, constantly improving.

6. Focused and effective portfolio management – a funneling approach, and putting the resources in place

Every development project is an investment and, like stock market investments, these development investments must be carefully scrutinized and focused through an effective portfolio management system. Strategic portfolio management deals with the broader question of resource allocation. Put strategic buckets in place to correct the balance of projects in your portfolio and to ensure that resources go to the high-productivity areas and project types. Product roadmaps are a solution and they attempt to ensure that resources are earmarked for significant projects driven by your business strategy.

Tactical portfolio management, namely project selection, is also vital to improving NPD productivity and is achieved through a funneling approach in your Stage-Gate system. Start with many solid new product concepts, and successively remove the weak ones via a series of gates. Use the productivity index in combination with scorecards at gates for more effective project selection. The result is fewer projects, but higher value projects to the company, and a significant improvement in NPD productivity.

7. The NexGen Stage-Gate Process – a flexible, adaptable, scalable and efficient product innovation process

Move to the next generation or next evolution of a Stage-Gate system. The first step in this evolution is to *build the six principles* above into your current process. This step alone will improve NPD productivity significantly because each one of these principles is proven to be strongly connected to productivity improvements.

Next, view your NexGen Stage-Gate system as more than a process with templates, checklists and flow charts, but rather as a *philosophy or culture* that fosters new and desired behavior. The structure and content of your NexGen Stage-Gate process is a *vehicle for change* – for changing the way people think, act, decide and work together. Define roles and responsibilities of players, develop a set of rules of engagement for gate-keepers, and provide training to effect these behavioral changes.

Make your process *scalable* to suit the needs and risk levels of different types of projects – Stage-Gate Regular, XPress and Lite – to handle large high-risk product developments as well as smaller, low risk and well-defined ones. And consider other versions of Stage-Gate to cope with other development projects, such as Technology Development, Platform Developments or Process Developments, that compete for the same resources.

Your NexGen Stage-Gate system should be *flexible, adaptable and dynamic* – adaptable to the changing situation and fluid circumstances of a project as it evolves, and to new information as it becomes available. Use spirals, as previously outlined, but also allow for team latitude (no activity or deliverable is mandatory), simultaneous execution, and overlapping stages by moving long lead-time activities forward.

Automate your Product Innovation process to accelerate projects and remove paperwork and administrative tasks. And build into your Stage-Gate system the necessary flexibility, capability and systems to work with outside organizations, building a network of partners, alliances and outsourced-vendors into the process.

Finally, and perhaps most important, *streamline your Stage-Gate system,* applying the principles of Lean Manufacturing with a focus on the value stream. Use maps of the value stream of typical projects along with retrospective analyses on completed projects (from the Post Launch Review). Identify time-wasters and inefficiencies, as well as weaknesses in the system. Determine what the cost of delay really is in the typical project – a dollar per day figure – and what these delays or inefficiencies are costing your business! Remove waste and inefficiency in your Stage-Gate system at every opportunity.

Moving Forward

Where does one start? A difficult question, and the answer will vary by business. But here are some tips and hints for moving forward based on our experiences in dozens of leading firms.

Senior Leadership commitment: The first step is executive or leadership commitment: first, that product innovation is vital to the future growth and prosperity of your business; and second, that excelling at product development and improving NPD productivity is paramount to the success of your business. You need a commitment from the top to move forward and to take concrete steps to improve NPD productivity. For example, at Procter & Gamble, one reason for their continued success in product innovation is their leadership. A.G. Lafley, CEO of the company, makes it clear: "Innovation is a prerequisite for sustained growth. No other path to profitable growth can be sustained over time. Without continual innovation, markets stagnate, products become commodities and margins shrink."[2] At ITT Industries, it was the entire leadership team of the corporation that endorsed the need for new products, and most importantly, made a strong commitment to improve new product development results for the company.

A Task Force: You cannot move forward alone… there is strength in numbers. So assemble a Task Force of key people but with executive sponsorship. These Task Force members should be representative of different businesses, functional areas and geographies. But most of all, they must have experience, insight and credibility in new product development. These are the people that are charged with identifying the major problems and deficiencies in your current product innovation practices and methods, and with developing and implementing the solutions. Ensure that at least some executives are members of this Task Force.

Diagnosis: Understand the problem before charging ahead. No doubt, some elements of our Seven Principles are already in place in your business. For example, you already do excellent voice-of-customer research, or already have a finely tuned system of gates in place. Good! But you'll also probably find at least some areas where there are deficiencies and gaps. Identify these. Listen to experienced project leaders and team members to find out what is going wrong and what needs fixing. Undertake some immediate Post Launch Reviews on recently completed projects, including a thoroughly retrospective analysis of these. And go through the value stream mapping exercise. Use the Seven Principles in this book as a benchmarking guide to best practices – how does your business measure up, how close do you come to embracing the Seven Principles, and what is missing?

Develop solutions: Your Task Force usually is able to spot problems, deficiencies and gaps in your Product Innovation process and practices. With some discussion, solutions are usually fairly evident. Again, use the Seven Principles in the last chapters as a guide. Many proven solutions and practices have been mapped out in this book for you and your Task Force. So be sure to review each principle with the idea of building it into your solution and methodology. And do not forget an implementation plan. Your executive sponsors want to see how the solution will be implemented, namely the next steps that they are expected to approve.

Implementation: At this point, the Task Force presents its findings, conclusions and recommended solutions to the executive sponsors for approval. Implementation is next, and the expectation is that the Task Force has mapped out a solid implementation plan for the executive sponsors to review and approve.

Do Move Forward

Now that you have finished reading this book, share it and discuss it with your colleagues. Whatever the outcome of your discussions with them, however, do move forward! The costs of standing still, coupled with the gains in productivity that are within your grasp, are just too high to permit inaction. Now, armed with the Seven Principles, make a commitment to take the next step towards *Lean, Rapid and Profitable New Product Development.*

How Toyota Uses Their Seven
Principles of Lean NPD[1]

1. A holistic, systems approach to product development:
- The basic elements of the product development system (people, processes, and technology) are fully integrated, aligned and designed to be mutually supportive.
- Highly skilled, intelligently organized people are the heart of the product development system.
- Processes are designed to minimize waste and maximize the capability of the people who use them.
- Technology must be right-sized, solution focused, and selected to enhance the performance of the people and the process.
- When these fundamental system elements are coherent by design, they combine to create a truly synergistic system effect.
- To achieve this result, other functions within the organization must also be aligned.

2. An imbedded customer-first approach:

- Truly internalizing this philosophy acts as the bond that creates a seamless integration between both functional specialties and fundamental system elements.
- The customer-first philosophy results in a deep understanding of customer-defined value which is the first step in any product development process.
- All system participants must understand customer-defined value from the start.
- Product development must deliver a product design that both meets customer needs and is capable of efficient manufacture.

3. A front-loaded process:

- Early engineering rigor, problem solving and designed-in countermeasures, along with true cross-functional participation, are key to maximizing the effectiveness of the product development process.
- By effectively segregating this inherently "noisy" phase of the product development process from the execution phase, Toyota is able to minimize downstream process variation that is crucial to both speed and quality.

4. Built-in learning and continuous improvement:

- Learning and continuous improvement are fundamental components of every job performed, rather than a special corporate initiative.
- Toyota accomplishes this by setting increasingly rigorous performance goals for every project.
- Both real-time and post-mortem learning events (called Hansai or reflection) are held that encourage functional specialists to validate and update their own knowledge databases.
- Learning and continuous improvement are also embodied in a problem solving process that creates multiple potential solutions and focuses on root cause countermeasures designed to stop future recurrence.

5. Synchronize processes for simultaneous execution:

- Truly effective concurrent engineering requires that each subsequent function maximize the utility of the stable information available from the previous function as it becomes available.
- Development teams must do the most they can with only that portion of the design data that is not likely to change.
- Otherwise, working with early data will result in tremendous waste and require a longer duration than a linear process.
- Each function's processes are designed to move forward simultaneously building around stable data as it becomes available.
- This practice is called "simultaneous execution".

6. Rigorous standardization to create strategic flexibility:

- This seeming paradox is at the heart of Toyota's quality and efficiency by creating far more predictable quality and timing outcomes.
- This principle includes concepts and tools such as reusability, common architecture, and standard processes – it is crucial in driving waste out of the product development process.
- Standardized skills, design standards and standard processes allow for specific program customization, broader scope of individual responsibility, a Just-in-Time (JIT) human resource strategy, flexible product development capacities and many other system benefits.
- These standards are also crucial to downstream lean manufacturing capabilities.

7. Go-to-the-source engineering:

- In this day of high tech engineering, it is very tempting for engineers to divide their time equally between conference rooms and their cubicles.
- "An engineer should never be more than a stone's throw away from the physical product". Source: Kelly Johnson, the famous head of Lockheed's legendary Skunk Works.

- At Toyota this philosophy is referred to as "Gentchi Genbutsu" and is practiced in many ways.
- Examples of this philosophy in action include spending a significant amount of pre-program time at manufacturing plants and dealerships, by working on competitor tear downs, or by personally fitting parts on prototypes.

ENDNOTES

Chapter 1

1. Arthur D. Little. *How Companies Use Innovation to Improve Profitability and Growth.* Innovation Excellence study, 2005.

2. The APQC major benchmarking investigation was undertaken by R.G. Cooper, S.J. Edgett, and E.J. Kleinschmidt. See *Best Practices in Product Development: What Distinguishes Top Performers,* at www.prod-dev.com and *Improving New Product Development Performance and Practices* by APQC. This study is referred to throughout this book as the "Cooper-Edgett-Kleinschmidt study" and abbreviated to the "CEK study".

3. Previous research by the authors and their colleagues that laid the foundation for this book is summarized in: R.G. Cooper, Chapter 1, "New products: what separates the winners from the losers", in *PDMA Handbook for New Product Development,* 2nd edition, New York, NY: John Wiley & Sons Inc, 2004; R.G. Cooper, *Winning at New Products: Accelerating the Process from Idea to Launch,* 3rd edition. Reading, Cambridge: Perseus Publishing 2001; R.G. Cooper, "Doing it right – winning with new

products," *Ivey Business Journal,* July-August 2000, pp. 54-60 (available at www.stage-gate.com); R.G. Cooper, "New Product Development", in: *International Encyclopedia of Business & Management: Encyclopedia of Marketing, First Edition,* ed. by M. J. Baker, International Thomson Business Press, London, UK, 1999, pp. 342-355.

4. *The PDMA Foundation's 2004 Comparative Performance Assessment Study (CPAS).* Product Development Management Association Foundation.

5. B. O'Reilly, "Secrets of America's most admired corporations: new ideas, new products", *Fortune,* March 3, 1997, pp. 60-66.

6. IRI InfoScan Reviews, *New Product Launches February 2003-January 2004.* Washington: Industrial Research Institute, 2004.

7. Source of data: Arthur D. Little. *How Companies Use Innovation to Improve Profitability and Growth.* Innovation Excellence study, 2005.

8. *Innovation 2005,* Boston Consulting Group, Senior Management Survey, 2005.

9. CEK study, see endnote 2; see also: R.G. Cooper, S.J. Edgett and E.J. Kleinschmidt, "Benchmarking best NPD practices – I: Culture, climate, teams and senior management roles", *Research Technology Management,* Vol. 47, No. 1, 2003, pp. 31-43; also: R. G. Cooper, S. J. Edgett and E.J. Kleinschmidt, "Benchmarking best NPD practices – II: Strategy, resource allocation and portfolio management", *Research Technology Management,* Vol. 47, No. 3, May/June 2004, pp 50-59; and: R.G. Cooper, S.J. Edgett and E.J. Kleinschmidt, "Benchmarking best NPD practices – III: Driving new product projects to market success", *Research Technology Management,* Vol. 47, No. 6, November-December 2004, pp. 43-55.

10. CEK study, see endnotes 2 & 9.

11. Source of data: CEK study, see endnotes 2 & 9.

12. PDMA attrition curve data: A. Griffin, *Drivers of NPD Success: The 1997 PDMA Report.* Chicago: Product Development and Management Association, 1997.

13. Reasons for failure are based on research summarized in: R.G. Cooper, Chapter 1, "New products: what separates the winners from the losers", in *PDMA Handbook for New Product Development,* 2nd edition, New York, NY: John Wiley & Sons Inc, 2004; and: R.G. Cooper, *Winning at New*

Products: Accelerating the Process from Idea to Launch, 3rd edition. Cambridge, Mass: Perseus Publishing, 2001.

14. C.M. Crawford, "The hidden costs of accelerated product development," *Journal of Product Innovation Management,* Vol. 9, No. 3, Sept. 1992, pp. 188-199.

15. R.G. Cooper & S.J. Edgett, "The dark side of time and time metrics in product innovation", *Visions,* XXVI, 22, Apr.-May 2002, pp. 14-16.

16. Most of the conclusions regarding NPD problems and causes are based on several benchmarking studies (endnotes 2 & 3). An additional and rich source of information, particularly the anecdotal information which leads to more insight into the problem and possible solutions, is the results of "problem detection sessions" held in about 200 businesses over the last five years.

17. R.G. Cooper, "Your NPD portfolio may be harmful to your business's health", *PDMA Visions,* XXIX, 2, April 2005, pp. 22-26.

18. R.G. Cooper & S.J. Edgett, "The dark side of time and time metrics in product innovation", *Visions,* XXVI: 22, Apr-May 2002, pp. 14-16. The negative impacts of cycle time were first articulated in: C.M. Crawford, "The hidden costs of accelerated product development," *Journal of Product Innovation Management,* Vol. 9, No. 3, Sept 1992, pp. 188-199.

19. PDMA studies: M. Adams & D. Boike, "PDMA foundation CPAS study reveals new trends", *Visions,* XXVIII: 3, July 2004, pp. 26-29; and: *The PDMA Foundation's 2004 Comparative Performance Assessment Study (CPAS), PDMA Foundation.* For mid 1990s data, see: A. Griffin, *Drivers of NPD Success: The 1997 PDMA Report.* PDMA 1997.

20. As reported in endnote 17.

21. Parts of this section are taken from: R.G. Cooper and S.J. Edgett, "Overcoming the crunch in resources for new product development," *Research-Technology Management,* Vol. 46, No. 3, May–June, pp. 48-58.

Chapter 2

1. CEK study; see Chapter 1, endnote 2.

2. Source: M. Adams and D. Boike, "PDMA foundation CPAS study reveals new trends", *Visions*, XXVIII: 3, July 2004, pp. 26-29; and: *The PDMA Foundation's 2004 Comparative Performance Assessment Study (CPAS)*. For mid 1990s data, see: A. Griffin, *Drivers of NPD Success: The 1997 PDMA Report*. PDMA 1997.

3. Section taken from: R.G. Cooper, "Your NPD portfolio may be harmful to your business's health", *PDMA Visions*, XXIX, 2, April 2005, pp. 22-26.

4. For 1985 data, see: R.G. Cooper and E.J. Kleinschmidt, "An investigation into the new product process: steps, deficiencies and impact", *Journal of Product Innovation Management* 3: 2, 1986, pp. 71-85. For current data, see R.G. Cooper, S.J. Edgett and E.J. Kleinschmidt, "Benchmarking best NPD practices – II: Strategy, resource allocation and portfolio management", *Research Technology Management,* 47:3, May/June 2004, pp. 50-59.

5. For more insights into this portfolio shift, see endnote 3.

6. Arthur D. Little. *How Companies Use Innovation to Improve Profitability and Growth*. Innovation Excellence study, 2005.

7. For more detail on the Productivity Index as a prioritization tool in portfolio management, see: R.G. Cooper, S.J. Edgett and E.J. Kleinschmidt, *Portfolio Management for New Products, 2nd edition*. Cambridge, Mass: Perseus Publishing 2002, pp 40-42.

8. Source: C. Fiore, *Accelerated Product Development*. New York, NY: Productivity Production Press, 2005.

9. Source of table: T. Jackson, *Beyond the pilot project: an essay on becoming lean*. The 4th Annual Best of North America Conference, in St. Louis, Missouri, Oct. 1999.

10. Source: N. Goyal, *Applying Lean Manufacturing to Six Sigma – A Case Study*, ISixSigma, 2005.

11. Metaphor taken from: T.R. Browning, "On customer value and improvement in product development processes," *Systems Engineering*, 6, 1, 2003, pp. 49-61.

12. T.R. Browning, endnote 11.

13. CEK study; see Chapter 1, endnote 2; see also endnote 3 in Chapter 1.

14. These published studies are in refereed, scientific journals, and hence meet more rigorous standards than many studies published by others. They are summarized in various publications; see endnotes 3 and 9 in Chapter 1.

15. M. N. Kennedy, *Product Development for the Lean Enterprise*, Richard V.A.: The Oakley Press, 2003. See also summary of University of Michigan study on Toyota, reported in: J. Morgan "Applying Lean Principles to Product Development", report from SAE International Society of Mechanical Engineers, 2002.

16. J. Morgan, see endnote 15.

17. See for example: M. N. Kennedy, endnote 15.

18. J. Messmer, "Increasing productivity with Lean development", Danfoss A/S internal company document, 2004.

19. Management Roundtable, *Apple Rethinks Core Process: Improves Cycle Time*, Knowledge Roundtable, Waltham MA, 2004.

20. Lean Product Development Group, *Roadmap*, 2005.

Chapter 3

1. For a good summary of success factors proven to drive NPD profits at the project level, see: R.G. Cooper, Chapter 1 "New products: What separates the winners from the losers," *The PDMA Handbook of New Product Development, 2nd Edition*. New York, NY John Wiley & Sons, 2004; and: R.G. Cooper, "New Product Development", chapter in: *International Encyclopedia of Business & Management: Encyclopedia of Marketing, First Edition*, edited by M.J. Baker, International Thomson Business Press, London, UK, 1999, pp. 342-355; and: R.G. Cooper, *Winning at New Products: Accelerating the Process from Idea to Launch*, 3rd edition. Cambridge, Mass: Perseus Books, 2001.

2. Source of data: CEK study; see Chapter 1, endnote 2.

3. Source of activities in a customer focused approach: CEK study; see Chapter 1, endnote 2.

4. E.A. Von Hippel, S. Thomke and M. Sonnack, "Creating breakthroughs at 3M", *Harvard Business Review*, Sept.-Oct. 1999, pp. 47-57.

5. Source: Kraft Foods case study found in the CEK benchmarking study; see Chapter 1, endnote 2.

6. Source of data: CEK study; see Chapter 1, endnote 2.

7. See endnote 1.

8. Source of data: CEK study; see Chapter 1, endnote 2.

9. Source of P&G example: R.G. Cooper, *Product Leadership: Pathways to Profitable Innovation*, 2nd edition. Reading, MA: Perseus Books, 2005, p 45.

10. As reported in: R.G. Cooper, *Winning at New Products: Accelerating the Process from Idea to Launch*, 3rd edition. Cambridge, Mass: Perseus Books, 2001, p 90.

11. Endnote 10, p. 59.

12. Source of data: CEK study; see Chapter 1, endnote 2.

13. Source of template: Stage-Gate Inc., www.stage-gate.com

14. Source of Toyota example: J. Morgan "Applying Lean Principles to Product Development", report from SAE International Society of Mechanical Engineers, 2002.

Chapter 4

1. Source: J. Morgan "Applying Lean Principles to Product Development", report from SAE International Society of Mechanical Engineers, 2002.

2. Source of data: CEK study; see Chapter 1, endnote 2.

3. Study undertaken by R.G. Cooper & E.J. Kleinschmidt, and summarized in: R.G. Cooper, *Winning at New Products: Accelerating the Process from Idea to Launch,* 3rd edition. Reading, MA: Perseus Books, 2001, pp. 58-64.

4. Quoted from: T.J. Peters, *Thriving on Chaos*. New York: Harper & Row, 1988.

5. Source of data: CEK study; see Chapter 1, endnote 2.

6. M. Mills, "Implementing a Stage-Gate® process at Procter & Gamble", Association for Manufacturing Excellence International Conference, "Competing on the Global Stage", Cincinnati, Ohio, October 2004.

7. As reported in: *Winning at New Products,* endnote 3.

8. *Accolade®* is a registered trade name of Sopheon Inc. *Accolade®* is a *Stage-Gate®* automation software package; see www.sopheon.com

9. Case studies reported by Sopheon Inc., developer of *Accolade®* – see endnote 8; claims are validated by the companies cited.

10. Source of data: CEK study; see Chapter 1, endnotes 2 & 9. See also R.G. Cooper and S.J. Edgett, "The Dark Side of Time and Time Metrics in Product Innovation", *Visions,* Vol. 26, No. 2, pp. 14-16, 2002.

11. Source of data: CEK study; see Chapter 1, endnote 2.

12. Source of data: CEK study; see Chapter 1, endnote 2.

13. Toyota example from J. Morgan, see endnote 1.

14. NPI is the acronym for 3M's stage-and-gate new product process.

15. Source of data: CEK study; see Chapter 1, endnote 2. A total of 51.7 percent of high-productivity businesses have a Stage-Gate® Process Manager versus only 23.1 percent for poor performers.

16. CEK study; see Chapter 1, endnote 2.

Chapter 5

1. Additional details of many of the portfolio methods outlined in this chapter can be found in two books by the authors. See: R.G. Cooper, S.J. Edgett & E.J. Kleinschmidt, *Portfolio Management for New Products.* Cambridge, MA: Perseus Publishing, 2002; and: R.G. Cooper, *Product Leadership: Pathways to Profitable Innovation,* 2nd edition. Cambridge, Mass: Perseus Books, 2005.

2. This chapter is based on a number of research studies and articles by the two authors and colleague, Professor Elko Kleinschmidt. See: R.G. Cooper, S.J. Edgett & E.J. Kleinschmidt, "Optimizing the Stage-Gate® Process: What best practice companies are doing – Part II", *Research-Technology Management* Vol. 45, No. 6, pp. 43-49, Nov-Dec 2002; R.G. Cooper, S.J. Edgett & E.J. Kleinschmidt, "New problems, new solutions: making portfolio management more effective", *Research-Technology Management,* 2000, Vol. 43, No. 2, pp. 18-33; R.G. Cooper, S.J. Edgett & E.J. Kleinschmidt, "New product portfolio management: practices and performance", *Journal*

of Product Innovation Management, Vol. 16, No. 4, July 1999, pp. 333-351 (winner of T.P. Hustad Best Paper award, 2000); R.G. Cooper, S.J. Edgett & E.J. Kleinschmidt, "Best practices for managing R&D portfolios", *Research-Technology Management,* Vol. 41, No. 4, July-Aug. 1998, pp. 20-33; R.G. Cooper, S.J. Edgett & E.J. Kleinschmidt, "Portfolio management in new product development: lessons from the leaders – Part I", *Research-Technology Management,* Sept.-Oct. 1997, pp. 16-28; and: Part II", *Research-Technology Management,* Nov.-Dec. 1997, pp. 43-52.

3. Source of data: CEK study; see Chapter 1, endnote 2. www.prod-dev.com

4. Source: M. Adams and D. Boike, "PDMA foundation CPAS study reveals new trends", *Visions,* XXVIII, 3, July 2004, pp. 26-29; and *The PDMA Foundation's 2004 Comparative Performance Assessment Study (CPAS).* For mid 1990s data, see A. Griffin, *Drivers of NPD Success: The 1997 PDMA Report.* PDMA, 1997.

5. Parts of this section taken from R.G. Cooper, "Your NPD portfolio may be harmful to your business's health", *PDMA Visions,* XXIX, 2, April 2005, pp. 22-26.

6. PDMA studies: see endnote 4.

7. For 1985 data, see R.G. Cooper. & E.J. Kleinschmidt, "An investigation into the new product process: steps, deficiencies and impact", *Journal of Product Innovation Management* Vol. 3, No. 2, 1986, pp. 71-85. For current data, see CEK study: R.G. Cooper, S.J. Edgett & E.J. Kleinschmidt, "Benchmarking best NPD practices – II: Strategy, resource allocation and portfolio management", *Research Technology Management,* Vol. 47, No. 3, May/June 2004, pp. 50-59.

8. For current portfolio breakdown data, see CEK study in Chapter 1, endnote 2. Source of 1990 breakdown: E.J. Kleinschmidt & R.G. Cooper, "The impact of product innovativeness on performance," *Journal of Product Innovation Management,* Vol. 8, 1991, pp. 240-251.

9. PDMA 2004 study; see endnote 4.

10. Section taken from *Visions* article, endnote 5. Data is from CEK study; see Chapter 1, endnote 2.

11. This section taken from R.G. Cooper, *Winning at New Products: Pathways to Profitable Innovation,* Microsoft Corporation whitepaper, 2005. Also avail-

able at www.stage-gate.com.

12. Parts of this section are taken from an article by the author R.G. Cooper, "Maximizing the value of your new product portfolio: Methods, metrics and scorecards", *Current Issues in Technology Management*. Hoboken, N.J.: Stevens Institute of Technology, Stevens Alliance for Technology Management, 7, 1, Winter, 2003, page 1.

13. Section taken from *Visions* article, endnote 5

14. See: *Visions* article, endnote 5.

15. Source of data: CEK study; see Chapter 1, endnote 2; see also *Visions* article, endnote 5.

16. Section taken from Microsoft Corporation whitepaper, endnote 11.

17. See: R.E. Albright & T.A. Kappel, "Roadmapping in the corporation", *Research-Technology Management*, Vol. 46, No. 2, March-April, 2003, pp. 31-40; also: A. McMillan, "Roadmapping – Agent of change", *Research-Technology Management*, Vol. 46, No. 2, March-April, 2003, pp. 40-47; and: M. H. Myer & A. P. Lehnerd. *The Power of Product Platforms*. New York: Free Press, 1997.

18. Section taken from Microsoft Corporation whitepaper, endnote 11.

19. Parts of this section are taken from an article by one of the authors; see endnote 12.

20. The Productivity Index is illustrated in more detail in endnote 1: *Portfolio Management for New Products,* pg. 40.

21. The real options or expected commercial value method is explained in more detail in endnote 1: *Portfolio Management for New Products,* pg. 42.

22. Source of scorecard criteria in endnote 1: *Portfolio Management for New Products,* pg. 54.

23. IRI study of portfolio management methods used versus results achieved. See: R.G. Cooper, S. J. Edgett & E.J. Kleinschmidt, "Portfolio management for new product development: Results of an industry practices study", *R&D Management*, Vol. 31, No. 4, October 2001, pp. 361-380; R.G. Cooper, S.J. Edgett & E.J. Kleinschmidt, "Best practices for managing R&D portfolios", *Research-Technology Management*, Vol. 41, No. 4, July-Aug. 1998, pp. 20-33; R.G. Cooper, S.J. Edgett & E.J. Kleinschmidt, "Portfolio management in new product development: lessons from the leaders – Part I", *Research-Technology*

Management, Sept.-Oct. 1997, pp. 16-28; Part II, *Research-Technology Management,* Nov.-Dec. 1997, pp. 43-52. See also endnote 1: *Portfolio Management for New Products,* pp. 163-164.

24. IRI study of portfolio management methods; see endnote 23.

25. The typical best performing business relied on an average of 2.8 portfolio tools for project selection. Source: CEK study; see Chapter 1, endnote 2.

26. Trademark of Microsoft Corporation. Microsoft offers different levels of resource management software, including MS-Project, MS-Project Professional and Enterprise Project Management.

Chapter 6

1. *Stage-Gate*® is a registered trademark of the Product Development Institute Inc. See www.prod-dev.com. This section describing *Stage-Gate*®is based on material from many sources; see for example: R.G. Cooper, "Doing it right – winning with new products," *Ivey Business Journal,* July-August 2000, pp. 54-60; R.G. Cooper, *Winning at New Products: Accelerating the Process from Idea to Launch,* 3rd edition. Cambridge, MA: Perseus Books, 2001, pp. 129-143; R.G. Cooper, "Stage-Gate new product development processes: a game plan from idea to launch", in: *The Portable MBA in Project Management,* ed. by E. Verzuh, Hoboken, N.J.: John Wiley & Sons, 2003, pp. 309-346.

2. Source of data: CEK study; see Chapter 1, endnote 2.

3. Quotation taken from PDMA best practices study; see: A. Griffin, *Drivers of NPD Success: The 1997 PDMA Report:* Chicago, Product Development & Management Association, 1997.

4. Recent PDMA study; see: M. Adams and D. Boike, "PDMA foundation CPAS study reveals new trends", *Visions,* XXVIII, 3, pp. 26-29, July 2004; and: *The PDMA Foundation's 2004 Comparative Performance Assessment Study (CPAS).*

5. Source of data: CEK study; see Chapter 1, endnote 2.

6. We did not call the process "Stage-Gate" until the late 1980s. The term "Stage-Gate" first appeared in print in R.G. Cooper, "The new product process: a decision guide for managers", *Journal of Marketing Management* 3,

3, Spring 1988, pp. 238-255; and in R.G. Cooper, "Stage-gate systems: a new tool for managing new products", *Business Horizons* 33, 3, May-June, 1990. But earlier versions of Stage-Gate® had been outlined in previous publications; see for example the early concepts of Stage-Gate in R.G. Cooper, *Winning the New Product Game: An Empirical Study of Successful Product Innovation in Canada*, Faculty of Management, McGill University, 1976; and R.G. Cooper, "A process model for industrial new product development," *IEEE Transaction on Engineering Management* EM-30, 1, Feb. 1983, pp 2-11. The first edition of the *Winning at New Products* book really began the popularization of Stage-Gate; See R .G. Cooper, "*Winning at New Products.* Reading, Mass: Addison Wesley, 1986. *Stage-Gate®* is a legally registered trademark in a number of countries. See www.prod-dev.com.

7. This section taken from: R.G. Cooper, *Product Leadership: Pathways to Profitable Innovation*, 2nd edition. Cambridge, Mass: Perseus Books, 2005, Chapter 7, pp. 200-231.

8. See Exxon-Mobile Chemical case study, Appendix A, in: R.G. Cooper, S.J. Edgett & E.J. Kleinschmidt, *Best Practices in Product Innovation: What Distinguishes Top Performers*, Product Development Institute, 2003. www.stage-gate.com

9. Source: *Product Leadership: Pathways to Profitable Innovation,* 2nd edition. Cambridge, MA: Perseus Books, 2005, pp. 233-236.

10. Stage-Gate TD is a special version of Stage-Gate for technology development projects; see *Product Leadership: Pathways to Profitable Innovation* in endnote 7, pp. 233-236. There is also a version for platform developments (same source). For additional information see www.stage-gate.com.

11. Taken from: J. Morgan, "Applying Lean Principles to Product Development", report from SAE International Society of Mechanical Engineers, 2002.

12. See endnote 11.

13. This section taken from: R.G. Cooper, *Winning at New Products: Pathways to Profitable Innovation,* Microsoft Corporation whitepaper, 2005. Also available at www.prod-dev.com

14. *Accolade®* is a registered tradename of Sopheon Inc. *Accolade®* is a *Stage-Gate®* automation software package; see www.sopheon.com

15. *SG-NavigatorTM* is a standard best-in-class *Stage-Gate®* framework, available from Stage Gate, Inc. at www.stage-gate.com

16. A.J. Campbell & R.G. Cooper, "Do customer partnerships improve success rates?", *Industrial Marketing Management*, 28, 5, 1999, pp. 507-519.

17. Source: C. Fiore, *Accelerated Product Development*. New York, NY: Productivity Production Press, 2005, p 24.

18. For more information on value stream mapping, see endnote 17, pp 24-26.

Chapter 7

1. CEK study, see endnote 2 in Chapter 1. See www.prod-dev.com.

2. As quoted in M. Mills, "Implementing a Stage-Gate® process at Procter & Gamble", Association for Manufacturing Excellence International Conference, "Competing on the Global Stage", Cincinnati: Ohio, October 2004.

Appendix

1. Source: J. Morgan "Applying Lean Principles to Product Development", report from SAE International Society of Mechanical Engineers, 2002 (www.sae.org/manufacturing/lean/column/leanfeb02.htm)

INDEX

3M, 3, 88

Accolade, 78, 155
accountability, 31, 32, 69, 73, 74-75,
80-82, 83, 86-87, 91, 93, 95, 132,
143, 145, 161, 167, 168
action plan, 161, 162
actions, recommended and
mandatory, 136
A.D. Little *See* Little, Arthur D
A.G. Lafley, *See* Lafley, A.G.
alliances, *See* partnering and alliances
American Productivity and Quality
Center, 2
Apple, 34
assessments: business, 30, 51, 157,
166; competitive, 54; financial, 51,
119, 120; market size and
segmentation, 51, 57; preliminary
market, 50; source-of-supply, 50;
technical business, 30, 50, 157,
166; value-to-customer, *See also*
value-in-use analysis, 51
automation in product innovation,
132, 154-155, 163, 169; benefits,
154
automation software, 154

batch to flow, 25, 26
benchmark data, 108
benchmarking studies, 20, 23, 29, 98,
133, 165
best practices, 24, 82, 88, 92, 106,
136, 139, 142, 143, 154, 165, 171;
inventory of, 92
best practices studies, 20, 41, 165
Boston Consulting Group, 3
Browning, T.R., 27
business case, 139, 157-158, 166
business function, 31
business strategy, 37, 54, 103, 106,
111, 127, 168
business structure, 25, 70; lean *See also*
Lean Manufacturing, 25, 132;
traditional, 25
businesses; best performers, 32, 37,
38, 39, 40, 41, 42, 47, 49, 50, 53,
54, 55, 67, 69, 71, 72, 73, 77, 78,
82, 88, 91, 96, 108, 114, 132, 133,
142, 143, 145, 150, 160, 163
best performers vs. worst performers,
22, 23, 29, 38, 41, 48, 51, 54, 56,
59, 74, 75, 78, 80, 82, 96, 100,
106, 112, 120, 133; poor
performers, 40, 54, 73, 75, 143

189

Additional Resources

More resources are available to help companies achieve innovation success through our sister company, Stage-Gate International.

For more information on ordering books, other products and services, please contact us:

Website: www.stage-gate.com
Tel: +1-905-304-8797
Email: info@stage-gate.com

Advance your awareness and understanding of the world's most effective product innovation practices. Join the Stage-Gate® knowledge community at www.stage-gate.com to receive the latest information on articles, research, and updates to keep you on the cutting edge of product innovation.

All books are available for purchase at
www.stage-gate.com

Presented through the Product Development Institute's
sister company, Stage-Gate International, seminars and workshops are
offered at varying times and locations throughout the year.

Attend Our Public Seminars

Seminar Topics and a Brief Description

Developing a Product Innovation Strategy and Deciding Your New Product Portfolio:
Making Strategic Choices and Picking the Winners

Picking the right projects and platforms to invest in is at the heart of successful product innovation. But effective project selections or portfolio management hinges on having a clearly defined and articulated product innovation and technology strategy for your business; the markets, technologies or products you should focus your efforts on and a strong link to portfolio management. Most businesses lack an effective and clearly articulated product innovation strategy; yet having this strategy is one of the important common denominators of successful businesses. Join Dr. Cooper and learn how to ensure scarce resources are consistently allocated to the most meritorious and strategic projects.

Successfully Designing and Implementing the Stage-Gate® Process:
A Best Practice Approach

The Stage-Gate Innovation Process is the world's most widely used method for taking new product ideas from inception through to successful launch – because it works! The critical challenge is not in the decision to adopt Stage-Gate but in how you implement it so it becomes engrained in the very fabric of your organization. Join Dr. Robert Cooper and our Principal Consultants at Stage-Gate International, and learn how to implement the Stage-Gate Process to realize its fullest potential.

Visit us online at www.stage-gate.com for more information and to register for the seminar that will help you to achieve profitable and successful product innovation.

Stage-Gate® Innovation:
Advanced Techniques for Accelerating the New Product Process for Maximum Productivity

Throwing more resources and money at your new product pipeline will not guarantee success; numerous studies have shown that there is no proven link between increased spending and success. Research has proven that one of the most important drivers of product innovation success is your product innovation process. The better your process, the better your results. Join Dr. Cooper for this executive seminar and learn new and advanced techniques every organization should incorporate into their new product process to realize top performance.

Generating Breakthrough New Product Ideas:
Feeding the Innovation Funnel

Product innovations are the life blood of the modern corporation. But product innovation is in trouble – R&D productivity is down – there is less bang-for-buck. Game-changing or blockbuster product innovations are absent in most firms' development portfolios. And the key role of innovation has not gone unnoticed by the financial community; their message is clear... organic growth, based on product innovation, is paramount. Join Dr. Cooper for this critical seminar on sustaining organic growth through product innovation.

Stage-Gate® Innovation Summit:
Leaders in Innovation Presenting Real Case Examples

Join Dr. Robert Cooper and Dr. Scott Edgett – the world's foremost experts in the field of product innovation – at the Stage-Gate® Innovation Summit for a powerful exchange of cutting-edge ideas, discussions and learnings with industry's best and brightest innovation leaders. Learn from case studies hand-selected for their rich, practical and exemplary demonstrations of product leadership and best practices. Discover how and why certain companies are achieving stellar organic growth results despite the numerous challenges and obstacles before them. Gain an instant, high caliber network of innovation professionals who make it their business to excel in Stage-Gate Innovation Processes. If product innovation is a critical business activity in your organization and you have adopted Stage-Gate Best Practices (or are about to), Stage-Gate Innovation Summit is a must-attend event.

www.stage-gate.com

Other Best Selling Books and Reports On Innovation

Generating Breakthrough New Product Ideas
Feeding The Innovation Funnel

Generating Breakthrough New Product Ideas, explains how to improve your innovation funnel with a steady stream of breakthrough new product ideas, providing numerous examples of the methods, approaches and techniques used by leading companies. Learn more about the impact you can make by leveraging an innovation strategy, voice-of-customer research, external ideas via open innovation, employees' creative talent, and fundamental research. Establish a proactive Discovery Stage that focuses on the drivers of innovation performance to transform your organization into an innovation machine.

Product Leadership
Pathways To Profitable Innovation (Second Edition)

Product Leadership, Second Edition, is the advanced course – a comprehensive guide for executives and senior managers who have a mandate to grow their businesses and impact performance through product innovation. *Product Leadership* goes beyond explaining what strategies are helpful to a company's success. It explores how to chart a competitive strategy and foster a culture that encourages product innovation. This book showcases examples of how companies such as Microsoft, GE, Nike and many others consistently prosper and it provides the reader with a wealth of practical knowledge.

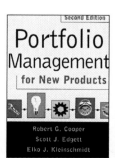

Portfolio Management For New Products
(Second Edition)

Portfolio Management, Second Edition, forces the reader to take a look at "the big picture" and question whether their organization is meeting its new product goals. This ground-breaking book presents a rigorous and practical approach to managing an organization's product portfolio and provides true examples of companies' portfolio strategies. It provides a wealth of knowledge, including how to pick the right approach for your organization and how to balance and maximize the value of your portfolio. This book is an essential resource for any company.

Winning At New Products
Accelerating The Process From Idea To Launch (**Third Edition**)

For over a decade, Dr. Robert G. Cooper's book has served as a bible for product developers' world-wide. In this fully updated and expanded edition, Dr. Cooper demonstrates with compelling evidence why consistent product development is so vital to corporate growth and how to maximize your chances for success. With *Winning at New Products*, you will learn methods for developing a Stage-Gate® Process, screening and prioritizing new product projects, incorporating customer input into product design, and much more to accelerate your speed-to-market.

Product Development For The Service Sector

In *Product Development for the Service Sector*, a comprehensive approach to product development tailored specifically for the dynamics of the service industries is presented, leveraging the extensive research and consulting experiences of Dr. Robert Cooper and Dr. Scott Edgett. Their experiences with companies such as Sprint, the Pennsylvania Energy Company, Marriott, VISA and the Royal Bank of Canada are highlighted.

Best Practices In Product Innovation
What Distinguishes The Top Performers

Best Practices in Product Innovation is a breakthrough study that reveals the impact of performance drivers at the business unit level. Authored by Dr. Robert G. Cooper, Dr. Scott J. Edgett and Dr. Elko J. Kleinschmidt, the foremost world experts in product innovation, this report provides five in-depth case studies of top performing companies, isolates the drivers of innovation strategy, outlines metrics used to measure new product process and practices, and much more.